Dwayne's Guitar Lessons Presents:

Learn Guitar Scale Theory

By

Dwayne Jenkins

Introduction

Learning guitar scale theory is an essential step for any guitarist looking to enhance their understanding and improve their playing skills. This book is designed to guide you through the intricacies of guitar scales and the theory behind them.

The journey of learning guitar scale theory can be an exciting experience, regardless of your skill level. Whether you're a beginner or an experienced player, it can help you unlock the full potential of your guitar playing.

This foundational knowledge serves as a gateway to better creativity, technical proficiency, and a greater appreciation for music as an art form. By knowing guitar scale theory, you will be able to enhance your musical landscape.

This sacred knowledge provides the structural framework upon which riffs, solos, harmonies, and melodies are built. By learning guitar scales, you gain the ability to navigate the fretboard and unlock its mysteries with confidence.

Allowing you to craft expressive musical narratives that will resonate with both you and your audience. Scales serve as the building blocks of music, offering a consistent language in which you and other musicians can communicate.

This book offers guidance and provides the keys necessary to unlock the hidden formulas of the notes that are used to create not only melodies, but also chords and progressions that coexist in harmony.

In addition, this informative training course will teach you about exploring the seven modes of the major scale and adapting to various musical genres. Very much like a chameleon that adapts to its ever-changing environment.

Through step-by-step instructions, diagrams, notation, exercises, and learning assessments, you will develop a comprehensive understanding of techniques and concepts associated with playing guitar scales.

That is, if you study and practice daily as recommended. All a person really needs to progress at anything is the desire to learn and the time to put in the work. Is that you? If so, this training course will get you where you need to go.

So, set your goal, get your practice time together, and set foot on the journey of learning guitar scale theory. You'll soon discover an amazing world of new possibilities. Good luck, and don't forget to have fun.

Sincerely, Dwayne Jenkins 2025

Table of Contents

Introduction

Chapter 3 Minor Scales 37

Chapter 4 Pentatonic Scales 55

Chapter 5: Modes and Their Mystique 67

Chapter 1 Getting Started

Lesson 1: Introduction To Music Theory

Music theory is the study of the practices and possibilities of music. It is a framework that musicians use to understand, analyze, and create music. This is done by learning about the elements within it.

By exploring the elements that make up music, such as notes, scales, chords, rhythms, and melodies, musicians can gain a deeper appreciation for how music works. Allowing them to express themselves more creatively.

The Importance of Music Theory

Understanding music theory is crucial for several reasons:

- **A Foundation for musical knowledge:** Music theory provides the basic building blocks needed to understand how music is constructed. It helps musicians recognize patterns, structures, and relationships within music, allowing them to read and write music more effectively.

- **Improved Communication**: Knowing music theory allows musicians to communicate more effectively with one another. It provides a common language to discuss musical ideas, ensuring clarity and precision in collaboration.

- **Enhanced Creativity**: Far from being restrictive, music theory can actually inspire creativity by providing a vast array of tools that musicians can use to explore new sounds and compositions. By understanding the rules of music, musicians can learn how to break them in innovative ways.

- **Better Improvisation Skills**: For those interested in improvisation, music theory is indispensable. It equips musicians with the knowledge to understand and predict chord progressions and scales, allowing for more confident and expressive improvisation.

- **Increased Versatility**: Musicians who understand music theory can adapt to different musical genres and styles more easily. Whether playing classical, jazz, rock, or world music, the principles of music theory remain applicable, making it easier to transition between styles.

- **Personal Growth**: Learning music theory can be an enriching experience, contributing to personal growth and development. It challenges the mind, encourages discipline, and fosters a lifelong passion for music.

By embarking on a journey through music theory, you are setting the stage for a richer, more fulfilling musical experience. Whether you're composing new pieces, jamming with friends, or simply enjoying your favorite songs.

A solid understanding of music theory and the elements within it will enhance your appreciation and enjoyment of the art form and allow you to compose more creatively.

Lesson 2: The Musical Alphabet

The musical alphabet is the foundation of music theory, and understanding it is essential for any guitarist. Unlike the standard English alphabet, the musical alphabet consists of only seven letters: A, B, C, D, E, F, and G. These letters represent the natural notes on a musical scale.

However, music is not limited to just these seven notes. Between certain notes, there are additional pitches known as sharps and flats.

A sharp (#) raises a note by a half step (one fret), while a flat (b) lowers it by a half step. This results in a total of 12 unique notes in Western music, forming what is known as the chromatic scale, or the musical alphabet.

The Chromatic scale

The chromatic scale is a sequential arrangement of all 12 notes, each a half step apart. Here is how the chromatic scale is visually represented:

A A#/Bb B C C#/Db D D#/Eb E F F#/Gb G G#/Ab
1   2   3 4   5   6   7   8 9 10 11 12

Octaves

An octave is the interval between one musical pitch and another with half or double its frequency. In terms of the musical alphabet, an octave spans eight notes, from one letter to the same letter. For instance, from C to the next C is an octave.

Key of C Major: C D E F G A B C

On the guitar, octaves can be visualized as the same note occurring at different pitches across the fretboard.

Understanding octaves is crucial for recognizing patterns and shapes that repeat across the guitar neck, which is fundamental for playing scales and improvising.

Practical Application

- **Fretboard Familiarity**: Practice identifying each of the 12 notes on the guitar fretboard. Start from the open strings and work your way up to the 12th fret, where the octave repeats.

- **Ear Training**: Listen to each note and its sharp or flat counterpart to develop an ear for pitch differences. This will enhance your ability to tune the guitar and play by ear.
- **Scales and Chords**: Apply your knowledge of the musical alphabet by constructing scales and chords. Begin with simple major and minor scales and gradually explore more complex scales like the pentatonic or blues scale.

Understanding the musical alphabet and octaves is a critical step in mastering guitar scale theory. With this knowledge, you will be well-equipped to explore the vast world of scales and improve your overall musicality.

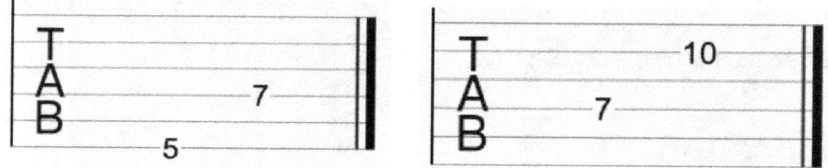

Here are a couple of examples of octaves on the guitar. If you're not familiar with tab, the 6th string (low E) is on the bottom, and the numbers are the frets.

Play these notes individually and listen to how they sound the same, just a pitch apart. Octaves.

Lesson 3: Intervals and Their Significance

Intervals are the building blocks of music, representing the distance between two notes. They are fundamental in the construction of scales, chords, and melodies.

By understanding intervals, you can gain insights into the relationships between notes and how they work together to create harmony and melody.

Half Steps and Whole Steps

Half Steps

A half step, also known as a semitone, is the smallest interval in Western music. It is the distance between two notes in the chromatic scale. On the guitar, this can be visualized as moving from one fret to the next on the same string. For example, moving from the 3rd fret to the 4th fret on the same string is a half step.

An example of this would be the G# to A, or the B to C. Two notes that reside right next to each other in the musical alphabet, or the chromatic scale.

Whole Steps

A whole step, or whole tone, consists of two half steps. It is the interval that spans two frets on the guitar. For instance, moving from the 3rd fret to the 5th fret on the same string is a whole step. Whole steps are larger than half steps and are crucial in forming the structure of scales.

An example of this would be the G to A, or the C to D, two notes with a fret in between them.

The Role of Intervals in Scales

Intervals play a vital role in determining the character and sound of a scale. The pattern of half and whole steps defines the unique quality of each scale.

For example, the major scale follows a specific sequence of intervals: whole, whole, half, whole, whole, whole, half. Understanding this pattern allows you to construct major scales starting from any note. Here is the C major scale.

C-w-D-w-E-h-F-w-G-w-A-w-B-h-C

This scientific formula works with all major scales. If you want to know what notes are in a scale, just follow the magical formula. Works every time.

Practical Application

- **Interval Identification**: Practice identifying intervals by ear and on the fretboard. Start by recognizing half and whole steps, then progress to larger intervals like thirds, fourths, and fifths.

- **Scale Construction**: Use your knowledge of intervals to build scales. Begin with the major and minor scales, and explore their distinct sounds.

- **Chord Formation**: Intervals are also key in forming chords. Understanding the intervals that compose a chord will help you in both reading and creating your own chord progressions.

Daily Exercises

1. **Fretboard Exploration**: Choose a note and move up the fretboard in half steps and whole steps. Listen to the difference in sound and feel the physical distance on the guitar.

2. **Interval Ear Training**: Play two notes in succession and identify the interval by ear. Begin with half and whole steps and gradually include larger intervals.

3. **Scale Practice**: Construct a major scale using the interval pattern of whole and half steps. Play the scale in different positions on the fretboard to become familiar with its sound and structure.

By mastering intervals and their significance, you will enhance your ability to understand and create music. This knowledge will serve as a powerful tool in your journey through guitar scale theory.

This will enable you to explore new musical territories with confidence and compose with a variety of concepts and techniques.

Lesson 4: The Major Scale Formula

Although we went over this briefly in the last lesson, I'd like to continue with it here in more detail. The major scale is one of the most fundamental elements in Western music.

It serves as the foundation for many musical concepts, including melody, harmony, and chord progressions.

Understanding how to construct and play the major scale is essential for any guitarist looking to deepen their musical knowledge.

The Major Scale Formula

Remember, the major scale is built using a specific sequence of intervals. Master these intervals, for they will set the foundation for all other scales to come.

Whole step, Whole step, Half step, Whole step, Whole step, Whole step, Half step. Do, Re Me, etc.

This pattern of intervals creates the distinctive sound of the major scale, which is known for its bright and uplifting quality.

Constructing the C Major Scale

As an example, let's construct the C major scale using the major scale formula:

1. **Start on C.**
2. **Whole step to D.**
3. **Whole step to E.**
4. **Half step to F.**
5. **Whole step to G.**
6. **Whole step to A.**
7. **Whole step to B.**
8. **Half step back to C** (octave).

As you can see, the C major scale consists of the notes **C, D, E, F, G, A, B, and C.** This scale includes all natural notes without any sharps or flats, making it an excellent starting point for beginners.

All major scales, no matter which ones they are, will have this same interval pattern. So make sure you know it well.

Playing the Major Scale on Guitar

To play the major scale on guitar, you need to become familiar with its pattern on the fretboard. Start by playing the C major scale in the open position:

In this example, you start on the 3rd fret of the 5th string (A), then play the 4th string open (D), and then the 2nd and 3rd frets on the 4th string. Then proceed through the 3rd and 2nd strings in the same fashion.

Practical Application

- **Fretboard Familiarity**: Practice playing the C major scale in different positions on the fretboard. Begin with the open position and gradually move to higher frets.
- **Ear Training**: Listen to the notes of the major scale and sing along. This will help you internalize the sound of the scale and improve your ability to recognize it by ear.

- **Scale Construction**: Experiment with constructing major scales starting from different root notes. Apply the major scale formula to build scales such as G major, D major, or F major.

Major Scale Exercises

1. **Scale Practice**: Play the C major scale up and down the fretboard, focusing on clean, even notes.
2. **Interval Recognition**: Identify the intervals within the scale. Notice the whole and half steps as you play.
3. **Transposing**: Choose a different root note and construct its major scale using the whole and half step pattern. Practice playing it in various positions.

Practice these exercises daily for maximum efficiency.

By mastering the major scale formula, you will unlock a crucial component of music theory that will greatly enhance your guitar playing.

This knowledge will enable you to explore new musical ideas and deepen your understanding of how music is composed. Enhancing your overall musicianship.

Lesson 5: Chapter 1 Quiz

In each lesson, I will provide you with a simple quiz to test your knowledge of what you have learned, or have not learned, within the chapter. If you miss something or don't know it, don't worry. Just go back and find it in the lessons.

This is a great way to make sure that you know the material and are ready for the next chapter. Have fun and good luck.

Q: What are the key benefits of understanding music theory?

A: _____

Q: How can it impact your creativity and communication?

A: _____

Q: How many unique notes are in the chromatic scale?

A: _____

Q: What are the roles of sharps and flats within the scale?

A: _____

Q: What is the distance of a whole step and a half step?

A: _____

Q: How do they contribute ot the construction of scales?

A: _____

Q: What is the interval pattern of the major scale?

A: _____

Q: How does it help to construct a major scale from the root?

A: _____

Q: Why is the C major scale a great place to start?

A: _____

Q: Why is it important to know note intervals?

A: _____

Q: How does the major scale set up a proper foundation?

A: _____

Q: What is the difference between the chromatic and major?

A; _____

Q: Why are exercises important in learning this material?

A; _____

By knowing the answers to these questions and knowing them well, you'll set the foundation of your education. The better your foundation, the better your guitar playing.

Chapter 1 Summary

In this introductory chapter, we have explored some essential foundational concepts. These serve as the groundwork for all your future studies. As you progress through this book, you'll continue to deepen your understanding and knowledge.

First, you explored the essential elements of music theory. Understanding these components provides the foundational knowledge for enhancing your musical communication.

Second, you learned the 7 notes of the musical alphabet and how the sharps and flats expand them to 12 unique notes, making the chromatic scale. As well as identifying octaves.

Third, you learned the concept of intervals, the distance between two notes, which are crucial for building scales. The role of scales, as well as practical exercises.

Fourth, you learned about the major scale formula. The scientific formula of whole steps and half steps, and how they can help you learn the notes to all major scales.

Lastly, you were introduced to a learning assessment. This is for you to make sure you truly know the material. Make sure to have fun with this.

Major Scale Examples

C-w-D-w-E-h-F-w-G-w-A-w-B-h-C = no sharps

G-w-A-w-B-h-C-w-D-w-E-w-F#-h-G = 1 sharp

D-w-E-w-F#-h-G =-w-A-w-B-w-C#-h-D = 2 sharps

A-w-B-w-C#-h-D-w-E-w-F#-w-G#-h-A = 3 sharps

E-w-F#-w-G#-h-A-w-B-w-C#-w-D#-h-E = 4 sharps

B-w-C#-w-D#-h-E-w-F#-w-G#-w-A#-h-B = 5 sharps

Notice how all these major scales use the same whole-step, half-step interval formula. By knowing this information, you unlock the mystery of the notes in each scale.

Also, notice that in this particular order, each one has one more sharp than the next. Be sure to use this as a reference guide when you need it. It will work wonders for your playing.

Chapter 2 The Major Scale

Lesson 6: Exploring The G Major Scale

The G major scale is foundational, often serving as a second starting point for understanding scale theory. The reason for this is that it has only one sharp or flat note in it. This would be the F#/Gb.

It consists of seven notes, just like the C major scale, and follows the same pattern of whole and half steps that was learned earlier, creating its distinctive, bright, and harmonious sound.

Construction of the G Major Scale

Interval Pattern

The G major scale is constructed using the same pattern of whole and half steps. This pattern is consistent across all major scales and tells you what notes are in any major scale. The notes change to hear the correct sound.

Let's take a look in more detail to this concept:

Key of C Major: C D E F G A B C

If you play these notes on the fretboard, you will hear the Do-Re-Me.

Key of G Major: G A B C D E F# G

Go through these notes, and you will hear it as well. The reason the F needs to be sharpened is to sound correct. If it were an F note, it wouldn't sound right. Try it.

This sequence of notes, G, A, B, C, D, E, F#, and G, comprises the G major scale, which is unique for containing one sharp or flat, making it the second most straightforward major scale to learn.

Practical Application

Playing the G Major Scale on Guitar

To get familiar with the G major scale on the guitar, begin by practicing it in the open position. Here's how you can visualize it along the 6th string, the Low E string.

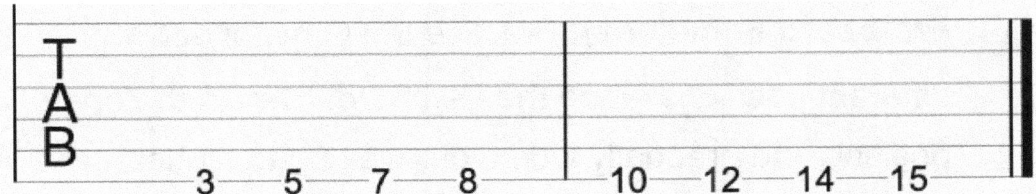

This is the G major scale along the 6th string. Remember, the
horizontal lines represent the guitar strings, and the numbers
represent the frets. Go through it and listen for the sound.

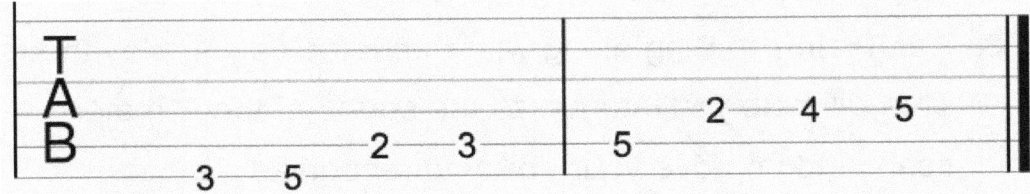

Here is another example of the G major scale. This time it is
played across the strings. Playing both of these examples will
help with getting familiar with the scale in different positions.

Anywhere you find the G note on the fretboard on any string,
you can play the G major scale. Also, notice the note intervals
in the diagram. They match the whole steps and half steps
you've been learning about.

Daily Exercises

1. **Fretboard Familiarity**: Practice the G major scale in different positions along the fretboard. Start in the open position and gradually work your way up to higher octaves.

2. **Interval Recognition**: As you play the scale, pay attention to the intervals between each note. Recognize the sound of whole and half steps, which will deepen your understanding of scale construction.

3. **Ear Training**: Sing along with the notes as you play them. This will help you internalize the sound of the C major scale and improve your ability to recognize it by ear.

4. **Scale Variations**: Experiment by starting the C major scale on different strings and in different positions. This will help you become more comfortable with the fretboard and improve your ability to navigate it efficiently.

By mastering the theory and construction of the G major scale, you add to your scale vocabulary. Serving as a valuable tool in your journey through guitar scale theory, enabling you to explore new musical ideas with confidence.

Lesson 7: Playing the C major Scale on the Guitar

Mastering the C major scale on the guitar involves more than just understanding its theory; it's about translating that knowledge into practical skills that enable you to play fluidly across the fretboard.

This lesson will introduce you to various techniques that will help you navigate the C major scale in multiple positions and patterns, enhancing your overall guitar proficiency.

Understanding Fretboard Patterns

To effectively play the C major scale across the fretboard, it is important to learn and visualize different scale patterns.

These patterns will help you play the scale in various positions, allowing seamless transitions and greater versatility in your playing.

Here are a few examples of how you can play this scale on the guitar.

24

Open position

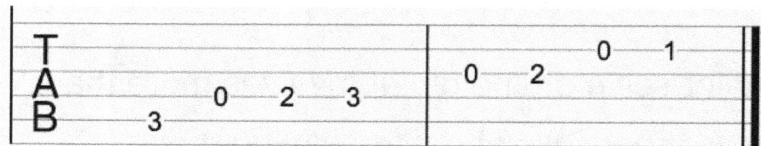

This is the most common way to play the C major scale on the guitar.

8th fret Position

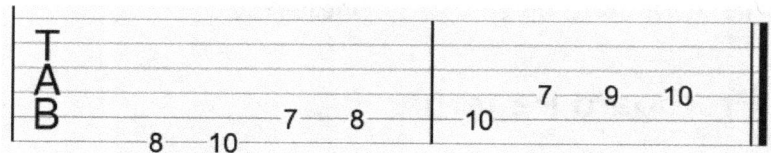

This is the same thing, but starts at the 8th fret on the 6th string. If you're not familiar with reading guitar tabs, the lines are the guitar strings, and your biggest string (Low E) is on the bottom.

Like the G major scale, practicing the C major scale in these two positions creates an excellent starting point for beginners, as one uses open strings, and the other starts further up the fretboard.

Remember, if you master the note intervals, this and all other scales can be played anywhere along the fretboard. No matter if it's C, G, A, or B. Just find the root note and go from there.

Techniques for Smooth Transitions

1. Finger Stretching and Dexterity: Consistent stretching exercises will improve finger flexibility and strength, enabling you to reach notes across frets without strain. Practice scales slowly, ensuring each note rings clear.

2. Alternate Picking: Use alternate picking (alternating downstrokes and upstrokes) to play scales smoothly and accurately. This technique increases speed and efficiency.

3. Position Shifting: Practice shifting positions by sliding your fingers smoothly along the strings. This will help you transition seamlessly between different scale patterns.

Practical Application

Daily Exercises

1. **Pattern Practice**: Choose one scale pattern and practice it slowly up and down the fretboard. Focus on clean notes and consistent timing.
2. **Transition Drills**: Move between two adjacent CAGED patterns, practicing the transition to ensure smoothness.

3. **Improvisation**: Use the C major scale patterns to improvise melodies. This will help internalize the scale's sound and improve creative expression.

While practicing, listen carefully to the sound of each note within the scale. Try to hum or sing the notes along with your playing to develop a strong aural recognition.

By incorporating these exercises, you'll gain greater control and confidence in playing the C major scale across the fretboard. This foundational skill will enable you to explore more complex scales and facilitate a creative approach to guitar playing.

Remember, this is the foundation of all scales. Why? Because it has no sharps or flats. Every other scale does, such as the G major scale learned earlier with the F# note.

Start with the C major scale, proceed to the G major, then go from there.

Lesson 8: Major Scale Patterns

Understanding and mastering various scale patterns is crucial for guitarists seeking to play the major scale fluidly across the fretboard.

We have already discussed this a little in the last lesson, but it will be discussed in more detail here. There are many ways to play scales along the fretboard.

Scale patterns provide a roadmap for navigating the guitar neck, enabling you to play scales in different keys and positions with ease. For this lesson, we will use the G major scale.

G Major Scale Pattern 1: Open Position

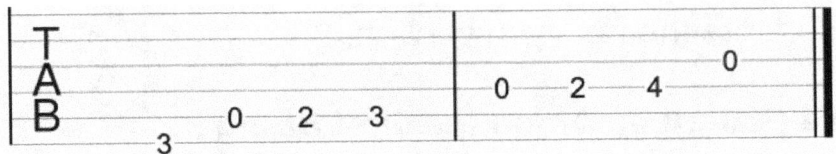

This is the most common scale pattern. Right by where the G major chord is played. Play it here to get familiar with this area of the fretboard.

G Major Scale Pattern 2: First Octave Position

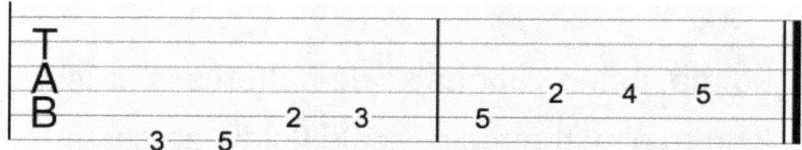

Here it is at the 8th fret on the 6th string and covers the first octave.

G Major Scale Pattern 3: Second Octave Position

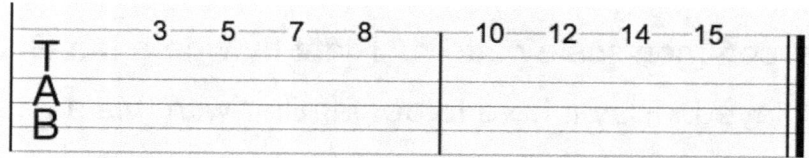

Here it is at the 5th fret on the 4th string and covers the second octave. Remember, the horizontal lines are the guitar strings, and the numbers are the frets you play on.

G Major Scale Pattern 4: Along the First String

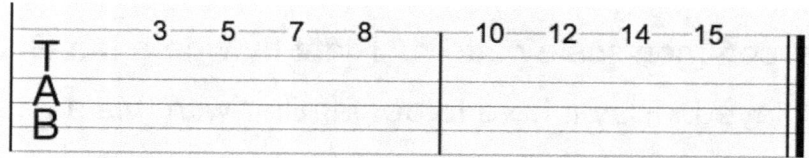

Remember, these are all the same notes.

Practical Exercises

1. **Pattern Isolation**: Focus on a single pattern and play it up and down the fretboard. Pay attention to finger positioning and accuracy.

2. **Pattern Transitions**: Practice transitioning between two adjacent patterns. Start slowly and aim for fluidity.

3. **Improvisation**: Use the major scale patterns to improvise short melodies or solos. This will help you internalize the patterns and develop creativity.

4. **Ear Training**: Listen to the notes within each pattern and try to sing them. This will improve your aural recognition and understanding of the scale's sound.

By identifying and practicing these common major scale patterns, you will gain confidence and versatility in your guitar playing.

These skills will serve as a foundation for exploring more complex scales and improvising across different musical genres.

Lesson 9: Application and Practice

Understanding the theory behind scales is essential, but the real magic happens when you apply this knowledge to your guitar playing.

This lesson focuses on practical exercises designed to help you seamlessly integrate the major scale into your musical repertoire.

By working through these exercises, you'll enhance your technical skills and develop a deeper connection with your instrument.

Exercises for Mastery

1. Scale Warm-Ups

Begin each practice session with a scale warm-up routine. This not only helps you get comfortable with the scale but also improves finger dexterity and coordination.

- **Ascending and Descending Scales**: Play the C major scale up and down the fretboard. Focus on smooth transitions between notes.
- **Tempo Variation**: Start at a slow tempo to ensure precision, then gradually increase the speed as you become more confident.

2. Scale Sequences

Playing scales in sequences helps you recognize patterns and improves your ability to navigate the fretboard.

- **Thirds**: Play the scale in intervals of thirds (e.g., C to E, D to F, etc.). This enhances your ability to identify and play melodic intervals.
- **Four-Note Patterns**: Practice playing four-note sequences (e.g., C-D-E-F, D-E-F-G) to improve your familiarity with the scale.

3. Chord and Scale Integration

Understanding how scales relate to chords is crucial for improvisation and songwriting.

- **Chord Tones**: Identify the chord tones (root, third, fifth) within the C major scale and emphasize them as you play.
- **Chord Progressions**: Practice playing the C major scale over common chord progressions like C-G-Am-F. This reinforces your ability to connect scales with harmony.

4. Improvisation Practice

Improvisation allows you to explore the creative possibilities of the scale.

- **Call and Response**: Create a simple melodic phrase (call) and respond with a variation (response). This exercise encourages experimentation and spontaneity.
- **Jam Tracks**: Use backing tracks in C major to practice improvising. Focus on creating melodic lines that complement the harmony.

Apply these concepts daily in your practice routine, and they will allow you to unlock hidden mysteries within the guitar fretboard.

5. Ear Training

Developing a strong ear is vital for recognizing scales and playing by ear.

- **Melodic Recognition**: Listen to simple melodies and try to replicate them using the C major scale.
- **Interval Singing**: Sing intervals from the scale (e.g., C to E, C to G) to improve your aural skills.

6. Creative Composition

Use the C major scale as a foundation for creating your own music.

- **Original Melodies**: Write a short melody using the scale. Experiment with different rhythms and phrasing.
- **Songwriting**: Incorporate the scale into a new song. Pay attention to how the scale interacts with the lyrics and chord progressions.

Tips for Effective Practice

- **Consistency**: Practice regularly to build muscle memory and reinforce the concepts you've learned.
- **Focus on Accuracy**: Accuracy is more important than speed. Ensure each note is clear and in tune.
- **Record Yourself**: Record your practice sessions to track progress and identify areas for improvement.
- **Stay Inspired**: Listen to music that features the major scale and draw inspiration from different genres.

By integrating these exercises into your practice routine, you will develop a more intuitive understanding of the major scale and its applications.

This will not only enhance your technical proficiency but also enrich your musical creativity, allowing you to express yourself more fully through your guitar playing.

Lesson 10: Chapter 2 Quiz

Here I present you with a quiz for chapter two.

Q: What is the interval pattern for the G major scale?

A: _____

Q: What type of distinctive sound does it produce?

A: _____

Q: List two techniques that can help you play the major scale.

A: _____

Q: What are two exercises that you can use in your playing?

A: _____

Q: What areas can you play the G major scale in?

A: _____

Q: What note is different in the G major scale?

A: _____

Q: Why does it have to be different than the C major scale?

A: _____

Make sure you know the answers to these questions.

Chapter 2 Summary

Chapter 2 delves into the fundamental aspects of the major scale, providing a thorough understanding of its structure and practical applications on the guitar.

First, you begin by exploring the C major scale, a cornerstone of Western music. You learned about its interval pattern—whole, whole, half, whole, whole, whole, half—which contributes to its bright and harmonious sound.

Second, you focused on techniques for playing the C major scale across the fretboard. By mastering various patterns, such as the open position and the 8th fret position.

Third, you learned about scale patterns. These were presented in the key of G major and provided different scale patterns to practice. Including open position, first and second octaves.

Fourth, you learned about practical exercises and techniques for integrating the major scale into your playing. Ideas such as warm-ups, sequences, and improvisational practice.

Lastly, you were presented wth a learning assessment as before to review your retention of the lessons. It is strongly suggested that you take it.

Chapter 3 Minor Scales

Lesson 11: The Natural Minor Scale

The natural minor scale is the alternative to the major scale, providing a contrasting emotional palette. While the major scale is often associated with bright and cheerful sounds, the natural minor scale imparts a more somber and introspective quality.

Construction of the Natural Minor Scale

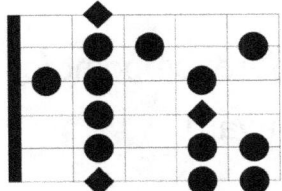

Interval Pattern

The natural minor scale flattens the 3rd, 6th, and 7th tone degrees of the major to give it a unique, melancholic sound. The interval pattern for the natural minor scale is as follows:

Whole step, Half step, Whole step, Whole step, Half step, Whole step, Whole step.

It has the same number of whole steps and half steps; they're just in a different order. Let's look at an example.

To understand this in more detail, let's construct the A natural minor scale, which consists of the following notes:

Key of A minor: A B C D E F G A

Now, let's look at the whole step, half step formula for this natural minor scale.

Whole step/half step: A-w-B-h-C-w-D-w-E-h-F-w-G-w-A

The A natural minor scale is often used as a reference point for learning other minor scales due to its straightforward construction and lack of sharps or flats.

It is also the relative minor to the C major scale because it is made up of the same notes. It just starts on the A note instead of the C. Take a look at the C major scale, you'll see what I mean.

All major scales have a relative minor that is made up of the same notes.

Significance of the Natural Minor Scale

The natural minor scale is essential for guitarists due to its versatility and emotional range. It is commonly used in various musical genres, including rock, blues, classical, and folk music.

By mastering the natural minor scale, you gain the ability to explore more complex musical ideas and convey deeper emotions through your playing.

Daily Exercises

1. **Scale Practice**: Play the A natural minor scale up and down the fretboard, ensuring each note is clear and even.
2. **Improvisation**: Use the natural minor scale to create simple melodies or solos over a minor chord progression. This will enhance your ability to express emotions musically.
3. **Composition**: Write a short piece of music using the natural minor scale. Experiment with different rhythms and phrasings to capture its melancholic essence.

Additional exercises

1. **Fretboard Familiarity**: Practice the A natural minor scale across different positions on the fretboard. Begin with the open position and gradually move to higher octaves.
2. **Interval Recognition**: As you play the scale, focus on the intervals between each note. This will deepen your understanding of the scale's construction.
3. **Ear Training**: Sing along with the notes as you play them to internalize the sound of the A natural minor scale. This will improve your ability to recognize it by ear.

By understanding and practicing the natural minor scale, you'll expand your musical vocabulary and enrich your guitar playing, equipping yourself with the tools to explore new creative possibilities.

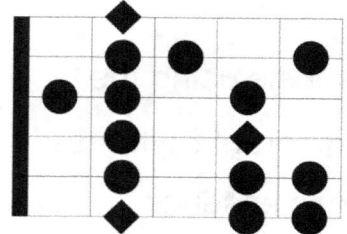

Play this at the 5th fret on the 6th string, and you will have the A minor scale. The major with a flat 3rd, 6th, and 7th note.

Lesson 12: The Harmonic Minor Scale

The harmonic minor scale is unique and captivating in Western music, celebrated for its exotic and dramatic sound. It is particularly popular in classical, jazz, and metal genres, where its distinctive tone adds depth and intensity to compositions.

Understanding the harmonic minor scale involves exploring its construction and recognizing how its differences from the natural minor scale can be used to create compelling musical expressions.

Construction of the Harmonic Minor Scale

Interval Pattern

The harmonic minor scale modifies the natural minor scale by flattening the 3rd and 6th notes only. This alteration creates a unique and recognizable sound.

Whole step, Half step, Whole step, Whole step, Half step, Whole step, and a 1/2, Half step.

Keeping the 7th note natural, it gives a 1 ½ step distance between the 6th and 7th notes.

To illustrate, let's construct the A harmonic minor scale:

A Major: A B C# D E F# G# A = no flats.

A Minor: A B C D E F G A = flat 3rd, 6th, & 7th.

A Harmonic Minor: A B C D E F G# A = flat 3rd, & 6th.

Notice how we kept the 7th note natural. By doing this, it provides a different shade of color to the minor scale.

The natural 7th note (G#) gives the harmonic minor scale its characteristic tension because of the step-and-a-half distance between the 6th and 7th notes.

Which resolves beautifully to the root note. Making it particularly effective for creating dramatic emotional music.

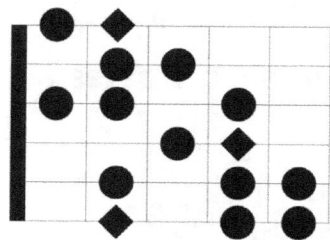

Play this at the 5th fret on the 6th string to get the A harmonic minor scale. Note the tone difference from the natural minor.

Characteristics of the Harmonic Minor Scale

The harmonic minor scale is known for its unique sound, which is often described as more exotic and evocative compared to other scales.

This is due to the augmented second interval (or minor third) between the sixth and seventh degrees, which contributes to its distinctive tonal quality.

This interval is unusual in Western music and lends the scale a sense of mystery and intrigue.

The harmonic minor scale is an invaluable tool for guitarists seeking to convey intense emotions and create dynamic musical narratives.

It is frequently used in compositions that require a sense of tension and resolution, making it a favorite among composers and improvisers alike. By mastering the harmonic minor scale, you will expand your expressive palette and unlock new creative possibilities.

44

Daily Exercises

1. **Scale Practice**: Play the A harmonic minor scale ascending and descending, focusing on smooth transitions and clear intonation.
2. **Improvisation**: Use the harmonic minor scale to improvise over a harmonic minor chord progression. This will help you explore its expressive potential.
3. **Composition**: Write a short piece or melodic passage using the harmonic minor scale. Experiment with different rhythms and dynamics to capture its dramatic essence.

By integrating the harmonic minor scale into your practice routine, you'll gain a deeper appreciation for its unique sound and its role in various musical genres.

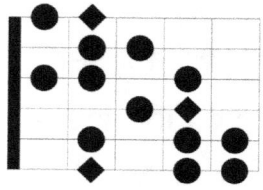

Remember, anywhere you play this along the 6th string will produce the harmonic minor scale. What fret you play it at will determine the key in which you play it.

Lesson 13: The Melodic Minor Scale

The melodic minor scale, sometimes referred to as the jazz minor scale, offers a unique blend of sounds that can be both expressive and versatile.

Unlike the natural minor and harmonic minor scales, the melodic minor scale has only one flat note. The 3rd. Keeping the 6th and 7th notes natural.

Construction of the Melodic Minor Scale

Interval pattern

This is actually easier to play than the harmonic minor scale because only one note is altered. Giving it a slightly different shade os color from the natural and harmonic minor scales.

This alteration gives the scale a brighter and more fluid sound when moving upward. The interval pattern for the ascending melodic minor scale is as follows:

Whole step, Half step, Whole step, Whole step, Whole step, Whole step, Half step.

Let's look at constructing the A melodic minor scale:

A Major: A B C# D E F# G# A = no flat notes.

A minor: A B C D E F G A = flat 3rd, 6th, & 7th.

A Harmonic Minor: A B C D E F G# A = flat 3rd, & 6th.

A Melodic Minor: A B C D E F# G# A = flat 3rd only.

This pattern creates the melodic minor scale, giving it a distinctive sound that is often used in jazz and classical music for its smooth melodic lines.

The 3rd and 6th tone degrees are flattened to make the harmonic minor scale, and only the 3rd note is flattened to make the Melodic minor scale.

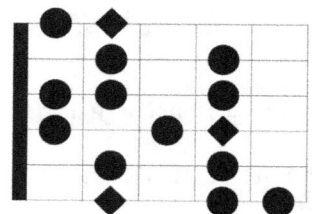

Play this at the 5th fret, 6th string for the A melodic minor scale. Compare its tone quality to the other two. Notice the difference between all three.

Playing the A Melodic Minor Scale on Guitar

To play the melodic minor scale on the guitar, you can start anywhere along the 6th string. Play it at the 5th fret, you play the A melodic minor. Play it at the 3rd fret, and it becomes the G melodic minor.

Daily Exercises

1. **Scale Practice**: Play both the ascending and descending forms of the melodic minor scale, focusing on clean and even note transitions.

2. **Improvisation**: Use the melodic minor scale to create solos or melodic phrases over a minor chord progression. Experiment with both forms to explore different emotional expressions.

3. **Composition**: Write a short piece or melody using the melodic minor scale. Try incorporating both ascending and descending forms to create contrast and interest.

By understanding and practicing the melodic minor scale, you'll expand your musical vocabulary and enrich your guitar playing,

Lesson 14: Practicing Minor Scales

Practicing minor scales effectively is crucial for any guitarist aiming to incorporate these scales into their playing repertoire.

Minor scales are incredibly versatile, offering a wide range of emotional expressions from melancholic to mysterious.

This lesson provides a series of exercises designed to help integrate minor scales into your guitar playing, enhancing both technical skills and musical creativity.

Here are the three minor scales you've learned so far:

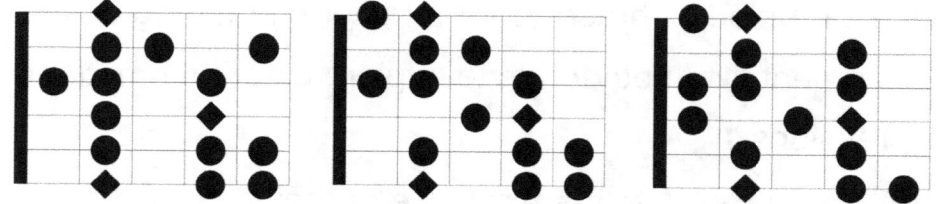

The **natural minor**, the **harmonic minor**, and the **melodic minor**. Study these and notice the different tone qualities that they produce. Then proceed to practice them until you know them thoroughly.

Additional Exercises

1. Scale Warm-Ups: Starting your practice session with scale warm-ups is essential for building muscle memory and agility.

- **Ascending and Descending**: Play the natural minor, harmonic minor, and melodic minor scales up and down the fretboard. Focus on smooth transitions and even timing between notes.
- **Tempo Variation**: Begin at a slow tempo to ensure accuracy, then gradually increase the speed as you gain confidence.

2. Interval Studies: Understanding intervals within the scales will improve your ability to recognize and replicate patterns.

- **Thirds and Fourths**: Practice playing scales in intervals of thirds (e.g., A to C, B to D) and fourths to enhance your ability to anticipate and play melodic intervals.
- **Sixths and Sevenths**: For more advanced practice, explore larger intervals, sixths and sevenths, which will further develop your understanding of the scale's structure.

3. Chord and Scale Integration: Connecting scales with chord progressions is vital for improvisation and songwriting.

- **Chord Tones**: Identify and emphasize the chord tones (root, third, fifth) within the A minor scale as you play.
- **Chord Progressions**: Practice playing minor scales over common chord progressions like Am-Dm-E7. This reinforces your ability to link scales with harmony.

4. Improvisation Practice: Improvisation allows you to explore the creative potential of minor scales.

- **Phrase Development**: Create simple melodic phrases using the minor scales. Start with short motifs and gradually build longer phrases.
- **Jam Tracks**: Use backing tracks in A minor to practice improvising. Focus on creating expressive lines that interact with the harmony.

Tips for Effective Practice

- **Consistency**: Practice regularly to build muscle memory and reinforce the concepts you've learned.
- **Focus on Accuracy**: Accuracy is more important than speed. Ensure each note is clear and in tune.
- **Record Yourself**: Record your practice sessions to track progress and identify areas for improvement.
- **Stay Inspired**: Listen to music that features minor scales and draw inspiration from different genres.

By integrating these exercises into your practice routine, you will develop a deeper understanding of minor scales and their application.

This will not only enhance your technical proficiency but also enrich your musical creativity, allowing you to express yourself more fully through your guitar playing.

The natural, harmonic, and melodic minor scales.

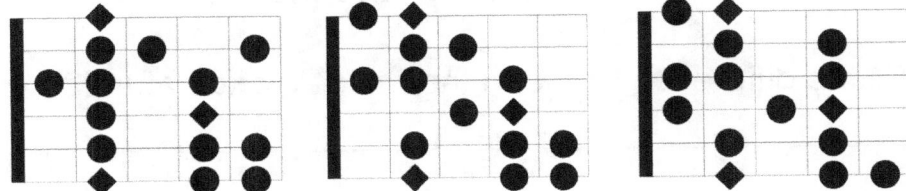

Lesson 15:   Chapter 3 Quiz

In this chapter, we have learned about the 3 minor scales that can be created from the major scale. Just alter a few notes here and there, and you've expanded your operation.

Q: What is the interval pattern of the natural minor scale?
A: _____

Q: How does it differ from the major scale?
A: _____

Q: Explain the difference between the harmonic and natural?
A: _____

Q: How does this difference affect the overall sound?
A: _____

Q: What note interval makes up the melodic minor scale?
A: _____

Q: What is the difference between the melodic and harmonic?
A: _____

Q: What is the difference between the melodic and natural?
A: _____

Q: How do you create the natural from the major?

A:: _____

Q: What notes are flattened in the melodic minor scale?

A: _____

Q: What specific notes make up the A major scale?

A: _____

Q: What specific notes make up the A minor scale?

A: _____

Q: What notes make up the A harmonic minor scale?

A: _____

Q: What makes the harmonic minor unique from the other two?

A: _____

Chapter 3 introduces three various forms of the minor scale: natural, harmonic, and melodic. Highlighting their distinctive sounds and applications. With study and practice, you will be able to incorporate these scales into your music.

Chapter 3 Summary

Chapter 3 delves into the intricacies of three minor scales, offering a comprehensive exploration of their distinctive sounds and applications.

First, you begin with an introduction to the natural minor scale. Learning about the interval pattern and its somber, introspective sound quality.

Second, you explored the harmonic minor scale. Learned about its note intervals and how the flattened 6th note gives it a unique tone quality.

Third, you learned about the melodic minor scale. Learned about its note intervals and how this creates a different shade of color from the other two minor scales.

Fourth, you learned about practical exercises that can help you to integrate these scales into your playing. Such things as warm-ups and interval studies.

Lastly, a learning assessment associated with these scales to help you develop a solid foundation for utilizing these scales in your musical repertoire.

Chapter 4 Pentatonic Scales

Lesson 16: The Major Pentatonic Scale

The major pentatonic scale is versatile and widely used in various musical genres. Known for its simple yet harmonious sound.

Comprised of five notes, the major pentatonic scale is often considered a subset of the major scale, and its structure makes it particularly effective for improvisation and songwriting.

Understanding the Structure

The major pentatonic scale is constructed by removing the fourth and seventh notes from the major scale. This omission results in a scale that is free of semitones.

This gives it a smooth and consonant quality. The interval pattern for the major pentatonic scale is as follows:

C Major: C D E F G A B C = 1 2 3 4 5 6 7 octave

C Major Pentatonic: C D E G A = 1 2 3 5 6

Now let's take a look at the C Major pentatonic scale pattern:

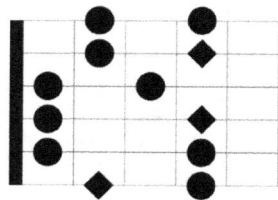

If you play this scale pattern at the 8th on the 6th string, you will have the C major pentatonic scale. The diamond symbols represent the root note. Notice how it repeats after 5 notes.

These 5 notes, **C, D, E, G, and A,** will produce a bright, open sound. Perfect for playing over a C major or A minor chord progression.

I chose to present this in C major because C major is the relative of A minor. Do you remember why?

It is because the two scales are made up of the same notes. This allows them to interact with each other nicely.

C Major: C D E F G A B C

A Minor: A B C D E F G A

Apply the same practice exercises as you did to the other minor scales to add this scale to your repertoire.

Lesson 17: The Minor Pentatonic Scale

The minor pentatonic scale is one of the most widely used scales in music. Cherished for its simplicity and emotive sound, it's known for its versatility and is a staple in genres such as rock, blues, jazz, and metal.

Providing a foundation for improvisation and composition, its five-note structure offers a straightforward and accessible way for musicians to create expressive riffs, solos, and memorable melodies.

Understanding the Structure

The minor pentatonic scale is derived from the natural minor scale by omitting the second and sixth notes. This results in a scale that is very easy to play.

A Minor: A B C D E F G A = 1, 2, 3, 4, 5, 6, 7, octave

A Minor Pentatonic: A C D E G = 1, b3, 4, 5, b7

Remember, to make the natural minor scale, you flatten the 3rd, 6th, and 7th notes. Hence, the flat 3rd and 7th notes.

Let's take a look at the A minor pentatonic scale pattern:

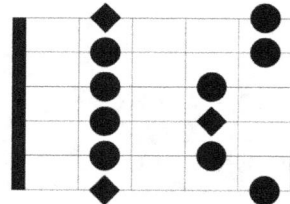

If you play this scale pattern at the 5th fret on the 6th string, you'll have the A minor pentatonic scale. Listen to how it sounds compared to the C major pentatonic.

A Minor Pentatonic: A C D E G = 1 2 b3 4 5 b7

C Major Pentatonic: C D E G A = 1 2 3 5 6

Notice how these two scales use the same notes. But because the A pentatonic is minor, it will have the flat notes taken from the A major learned earlier. It is these two flat notes that give it that dark sound.

Since the major pentatonic scale doesn't have any flat notes, it provides a nice, bright, uplifting sound.

Be sure to apply the same practical exercises for the other scales to the minor pentatonic and add it to your guitar scale vocabulary.

Lesson 18: Pentatonic Scale Patterns

Pentatonic scales are a staple in the toolkit of any guitarist, offering simplicity and adaptability across various genres.

To harness their full potential, it's essential to familiarize yourself with the 5 pentatonic scale patterns and practice them across the fretboard.

Since there are 5 notes in the scale, there are 5 patterns. These are based on each of the 5 notes in the scale.

C Major Pentatonic Scale: C D E G A

The C major scale patterns will be based on these five notes. Starting at the C note, proceeding to the D, E, G, and finally the A note.

A Minor Pentatonic Scale: A C D E G

The A minor scale patterns will be based on these 5 notes. Starting at the A note, proceeding to the C, D, E, and finally the G note.

The 5 Major Pentatonic Scale Patterns:

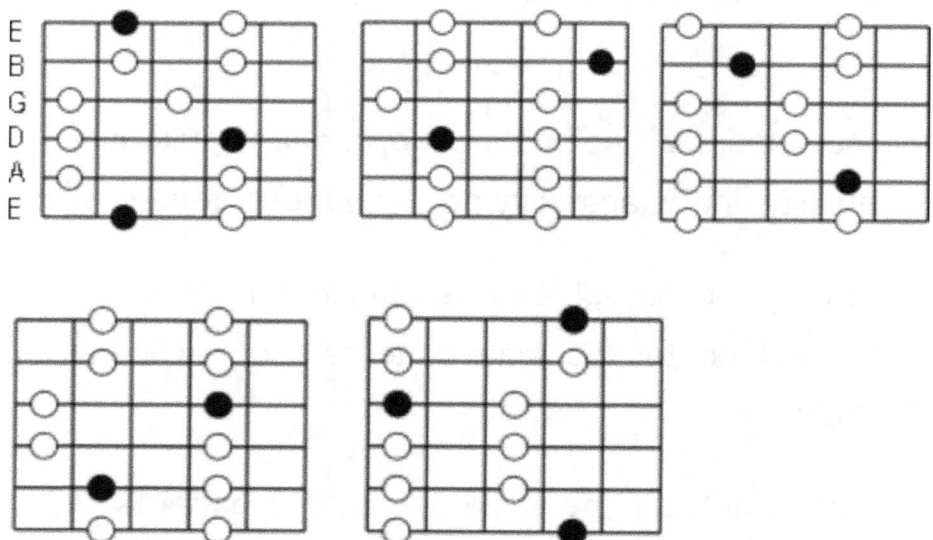

If you start these at the 8th fret (the C note) on the 6th string, you'll see that they line up perfectly with the notes of the C major pentatonic scale. **C D E G A**.

The 1st pattern starts on the **C** note (8th fret), 2nd on the **D** (10th fret), 3rd on the **E** (12th fret), 4th on the **G** (15th fret), and the 5th on the **A** (17th fret), which allows you to cover a whole octave along the fretboard.

By mastering these five major pentatonic patterns, you can build a roadmap along the fretboard,

The 5 Minor Pentatonic Scale Patterns:

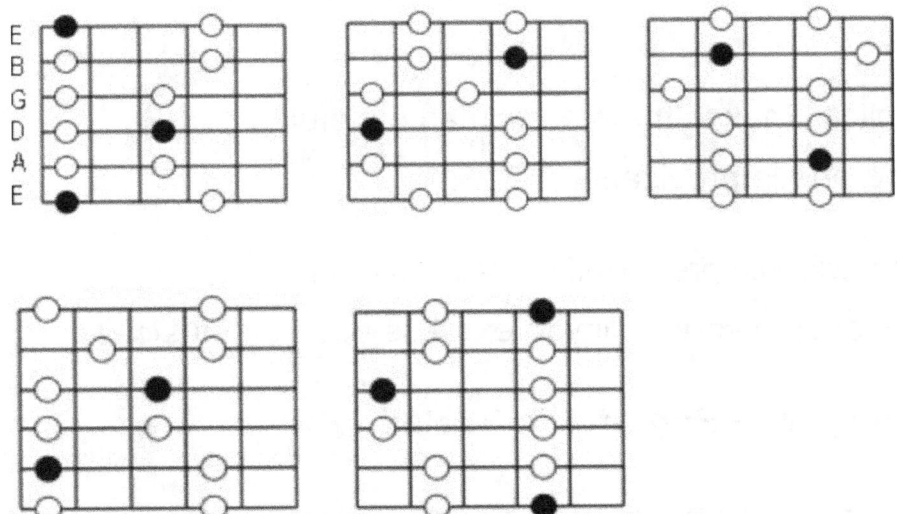

If you start on the 5th fret of the 6th string (the A note), you'll see that they line up perfectly with the notes of the A minor pentatonic scale. **A C D E G**.

The 1st pattern starts on the **A** note (5th fret), 2nd on the **C** (8th fret), 3rd on the **D** (10th fret), 4th on the **E** (12th fret), and the 5th on the **G** (15th fret), which allows you to cover a whole octave along the fretboard. Same as the major pentatonic.

Study and practice these patterns daily, as they will allow you to build a roadmap that will allow you to go anywhere you choose along the fretboard.

Lesson 19: Creative Pentatonic Applications

Pentatonic scales are a powerful tool for guitarists, providing a straightforward yet versatile framework for crafting melodies and solos.

Their simplicity makes them particularly useful in both songwriting and improvisation.

This lesson will explore creative ways to apply pentatonic scales, enhancing your ability to express yourself musically.

Songwriting with Pentatonic Scales

The pentatonic scale's five-note structure allows for the creation of catchy and memorable melodies with minimal risk of dissonance. Here are some tips for incorporating pentatonic scales into your songwriting process:

- **Melodic Development**: Use the scale to develop strong melodic themes. The absence of semitones creates a smooth and open sound that's easy to build upon.

- **Riff Creation**: Craft riffs and hooks using the pentatonic scale. Its simplicity lends itself well to repetitive patterns that can anchor a song.

- **Harmonization**: Experiment with harmonizing melodies within the pentatonic framework. This can add depth and complexity to your compositions while maintaining a cohesive sound.

Improvisation Techniques

Improvisation is where the pentatonic scale truly shines, offering a reliable foundation for spontaneous musical expression. Here are some techniques to elevate your improvisational skills:

- **Phrase Variation**: Start with a simple pentatonic phrase and experiment with variations. Change the rhythm, add slides or bends, and explore different articulations to create interest.

- **Call and Response**: Use the pentatonic scale to engage in a musical conversation. A phrase and response with a variation or contrasting idea, building a dynamic solo

Daily Exercises

1. Melody Construction: Choose a pentatonic scale and create a short melody. Focus on using different rhythms and dynamics to express a range of emotions. Record and refine your ideas, experimenting with variations.

2. Riff Exploration: Develop a riff using the pentatonic scale. Play it over a simple chord progression, paying attention to how the riff interacts with the harmony. Try transposing the riff to different keys to explore new textures.

3. Improvisation Practice: Jam over a backing track in a key that matches your chosen pentatonic scale. Aim to create cohesive solos by connecting phrases and exploring the full range of the fretboard. Record your improvisations and listen back to identify areas for improvement.

4. Modal Integration: Select a mode and pair it with a corresponding pentatonic scale. Practice improvising over modal chord progressions, using the pentatonic scale to guide your note choices and enhance your melodic lines.

By exploring the pentatonic scales, both major and minor, you will be able to unlock avenues of exploration and innovation.

Lesson 20: Chapter 4 Quiz

Understanding the concepts covered in Chapter 4 will provide you with a solid foundation for using the pentatonic scales.

Q: What are the notes of the C major pentatonic scale?
A: _____

Q: How do these notes contribute to its musical versatility?
A: _____

Q: What notes are in the A minor pentatonic scale?
A: _____

Q: How is this scale derived from the natural minor scale?
A: _____

Q: What is the benefit of learning the 5 pentatonic patterns?
A: _____

Q: List two ways to use the pentatonic scales in your playing?
A: _____

Knowing the answers to these questions will build a solid foundation of the pentatonic scales and allow you to master using them along the fretboard in any key.

Chapter 4 Summary

Chapter 4 dives into the wonderful world of pentatonic scales. Both Major and minor. Allowing you to develop a solid framework for riffs, solos, and improvisation.

First, you learn the C major pentatonic scale. What notes are in it, and how you eliminate the 4th and 7th notes of the major to create it.

Second, you learn the A minor pentatonic scale. What notes are in it, and by eliminating the 2nd and 6th notes, you create a scale that is easy to play and widely used.

Third, you learn all five pentatonic scale patterns and how they derive from each of the five notes of the scale. Allowing you to build a fretboard roadmap.

Fourth, you learn how you can effectively use them in your playing. To create catchy riffs, jaw-dropping solos, and memorable melody lines.

Lastly, you are presented with another learning assessment to help you judge what you know and what still needs to be learned. Mastering these lessons will allow you to enhance your improvisation skills.

Chapter 5 Modes And Their Mystique

Lesson 21: Modes Introduction

Modes are a fascinating and integral part of music theory, offering a wide array of tonal possibilities that can enrich your playing and compositional skills.

Originating from ancient Greek music, modes have evolved over centuries and remain a vital element in Western music, providing unique sonic landscapes that can transform a simple melody into something extraordinary.

What Are Modes?

Modes are scales derived from the major scale, each starting on a different note of the scale. While the major scale (also known as the Ionian mode) is the most familiar, there are six other modes, each with its own character and emotional quality.

By understanding and utilizing these modes, you can explore new musical textures and express a broader range of emotions in your music.

The Seven Modes

1. **Ionian**: Equivalent to the major scale, the Ionian mode is bright and happy, often used in a wide variety of music.

2. **Dorian**: Known for its jazzy and soulful sound, the Dorian mode is a minor scale with a raised sixth, offering a unique twist on the traditional minor feel.

3. **Phrygian**: This mode has a distinct Spanish or Middle Eastern flavor, characterized by a minor scale with a lowered second.

4. **Lydian**: With its raised fourth, the Lydian mode has a dreamy and ethereal quality, often used in film scores and jazz.

5. **Mixolydian**: Popular in rock and blues, the Mixolydian mode features a major scale with a lowered seventh, giving it a bluesy feel.

6. **Aeolian**: Also known as the natural minor scale, the Aeolian mode is somber and introspective, commonly used in various musical genres.

7. **Locrian**: The most unique of the modes, the Locrian mode has a diminished fifth, making it dark and unstable, often used for tension and dissonance.

Lesson 22: Ionian and Dorian

The Ionian Mode (#1 major)

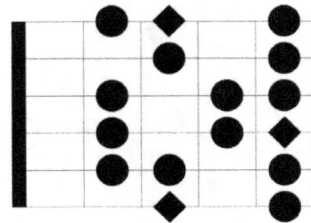

Characteristics

- **Equivalent to the Major Scale**: The Ionian mode is identical to the major scale, starting on the first degree of the scale. Its interval pattern is whole, whole, half, whole, whole, whole, half.

- **Bright and Uplifting**: Known for its cheerful and harmonious sound, the Ionian mode is often associated with happiness and positivity. It is the backbone of many Western musical compositions.

The Ionian mode is a great mode to use over any major chord progression. Since it has half-steps, it will allow you to create Melodies of a different nature than the natural major scale or the major pentatonic scale.

The Dorian Mode (#2 minor)

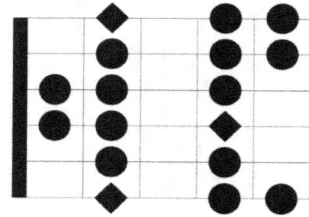

Characteristics

- **Minor with a Twist**: The Dorian mode is a minor scale with a raised sixth degree. Its interval pattern is whole, half, whole, whole, whole, half, whole.

- **Jazzy and Soulful**: The raised sixth gives the Dorian mode a unique, jazzy feel, making it both melancholic and hopeful. It is often used to convey a more complex emotional narrative.

Work on playing these modes in multiple keys. Focus on the different intervals that give them their distinct tonal qualities.

The Dorian mode is minor in nature, so it is going to give you another option for creating emotions similar to the other minor scales that you have previously learned.

Lesson 23: Phrygian and Lydian

In this lesson, we delve into the Phrygian and Lydian modes, each offering distinct tonal qualities.

The Phrygian Mode (#3 minor)

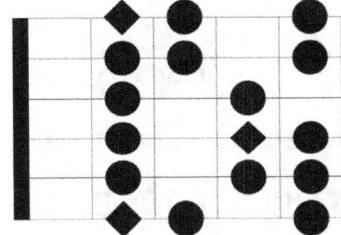

Characteristics

- **Spanish and Middle Eastern Flavor:** The Phrygian mode is known for its exotic and mysterious sound, often associated with Spanish and Middle Eastern music

- **Minor with a Lowered Second:** The Phrygian mode is a minor scale with a distinctive lowered second.

With the interval pattern being H-W-W-W-H-W-W, you produce a minor tone quality that is different from the Dorian mode.

The Lydian Mode (#4 major)

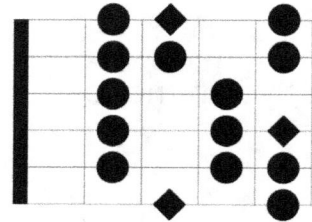

Characteristics

- Dreamy and Ethereal: The Lydian mode is known for its bright and uplifting sound, often described as dreamy or ethereal. It is characterized by a raised fourth, which contributes to its unique, floating quality.
- Major with a Raised Fourth: The Lydian mode is a major scale with a raised fourth degree. Its interval pattern is whole, whole, whole, half, whole, whole, half.

Since the Lydian mode is a major mode but with a raised 4th note, 1, 2, 3, 4#, 5, 6, 7, it gives it an uplifting tone that is slightly different from the Ionian mode and the natural major scale.

Lesson 24: The Mixolydian, Aeolian, and Locrian

In this lesson, we will explore the remaining modes: The Mixolydian, Aeolian, and Locrian. Each of these modes offers a distinct sound and character.

The Mixolydian Mode (#5 major)

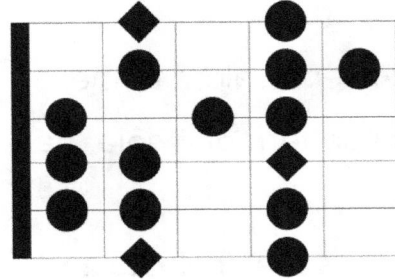

Characteristics

- **Major with a Twist:** The Mixolydian mode is a major scale with a lowered seventh degree.
- **Bluesy and Rocking:** Known for its bluesy feel, the Mixolydian mode is often used in rock, blues, and jazz. music.

Since the note interval is W-W-H-W-W-H-W, it makes it another major mode that works well in major keys.

The Aeolian Mode (#6 natural minor)

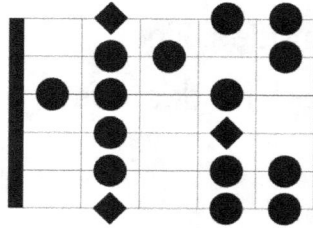

Characteristics

- **Natural Minor:** The Aeolian mode is equivalent to the natural minor scale, with an interval pattern of whole, half, whole, whole, half, whole, whole.
- **Somber and Reflective:** Known for its melancholic and introspective sound, the Aeolian mode is a common choice for conveying emotions ranging from sadness to introspection.

The Aeolian mode will always start on the 6th tone degree, and very important to master, because it will always work with a minor key or its relative major.

Remember, this scale has the flattened 3rd, 6th, and 7th tone degrees. The natural minor, as in A minor.

The Locrian Mode (#7 diminished)

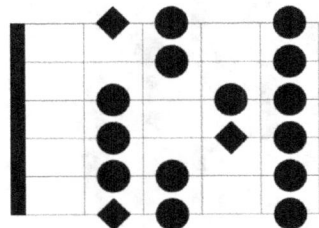

Characteristics

- **Diminished and Unstable:** The Locrian mode is characterized by a diminished fifth, with an interval pattern of half, whole, whole, half, whole, whole, whole.
- **Dark and Tense:** Known for its dissonant and unstable sound, the Locrian mode is often used to create tension and drama in music.

By mastering the Mixolydian, Aeolian, and Locrian modes, you'll complete all 7 modes within the major scale. These modes offer unique ways to enrich your compositions.

With these 7 modes, you'll not only enhance your knowledge of the major scale, but you will also be able to add to your scale vocabulary and improve your mastery of the fretboard.

The 7 Modes of the Major Scale

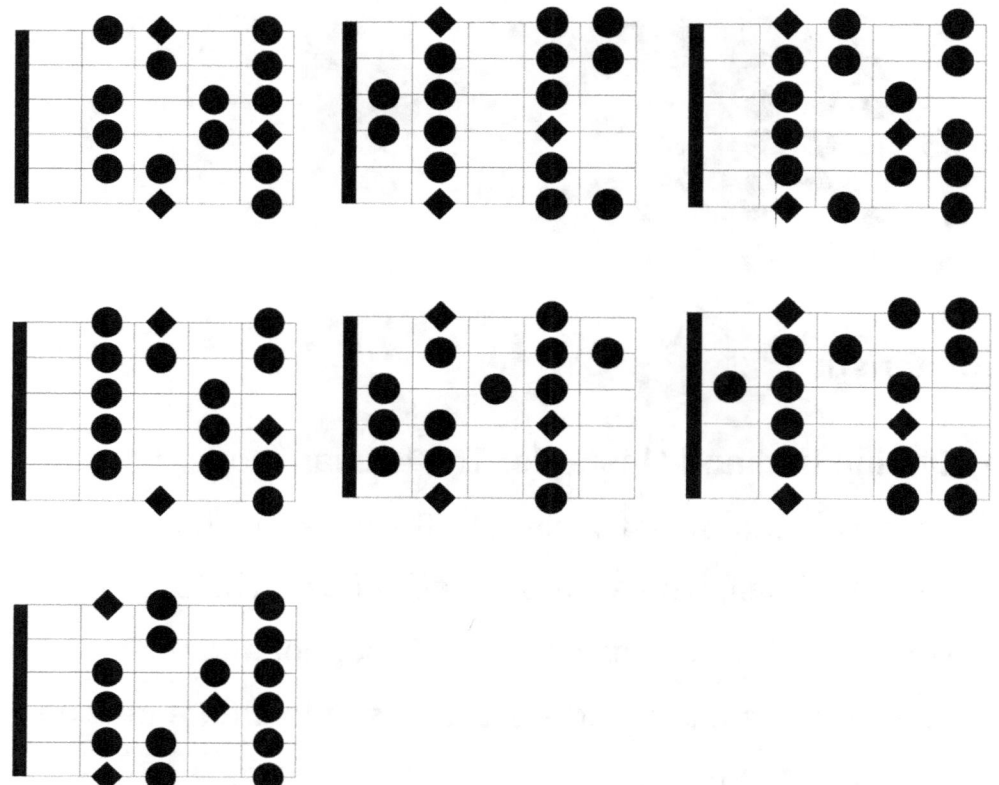

Here are all 7 modes that derive from the major scale. Be sure to study and practice them daily. Start in one key, master their locations, and then proceed to different ones.

These can increase your musicianship, fretboard mastery, and give you a wealth of options for creating musical landscapes of many colors and emotions.

Lesson 25: Chapter 5 Quiz

In this chapter, we have learned about the 7 modes of the major scale. These will be a great addition to your scale vocabulary.

Q: What are the 7 modes?

A: _____

Q: What are the Ionian and Dorian modes' characteristics?

A: _____

Q: What are the Phrygian and Lydian modes' characteristics?

A: _____

Q: What makes the Mixolydian and Aeolian modes unique?

A: _____

Q: What makes the Locrian mode unique from the others?

A: _____

Q: What styles of music are the modes commonly used in?

A: _____

By answering these questions, you will be able to reinforce your understanding of the concepts covered in Chapter 5, enhancing your ability to utilize modes effectively in your music.

Chapter 5 Summary

Modes are scales derived from the major scale, each starting on a different note, offering distinct sonic landscapes that enrich musical expression. From ancient Greek to Western music.

First, you are introduced to the modes, their origins, and how they are derived from the 7 notes of the major scale. Each starts at a different note.

Second, you learned about the Ionian and Dorian mode scale patterns and characteristics. The Ionian is also major, and the Dorian is minor.

Third, you learned about the Phrygian and Lydian mode scale patterns and characteristics. The Phrygian is also minor, and the Lydian is major.

Fourth, you learned the last three. Mixolydian (major), Aeolian (minor), and the Locrian (diminished). Allowing you to enrich the complexity of your music.

Lastly, a learning assessment on the modes. If you practice them daily, you will unlock a world of possibilities, as these can be used for both melody and harmony.

Chapter 6 Improvisation

Lesson 26: The Role Of Scales In Improvisation

Improvisation is a cornerstone of musical creativity, allowing musicians to spontaneously express their emotions and ideas through their instruments. Scales play a crucial role in this process, providing a framework upon which melodies and solos are built.

By understanding the role of scales in improvisation, you'll be able to craft compelling musical narratives and develop your unique voice as a guitarist.

The Importance of Scales in Improvisation

- **Harmonic Foundation:** Scales serve as the harmonic foundation for improvisation, helping you choose notes that fit well with the underlying chord progressions. By aligning your solos with the scale corresponding to the chords, you ensure that your improvisations are cohesive and harmonically sound.

- **Melodic Development:** Scales offer a palette of notes from which you can draw to create melodies. Understanding the scale's structure and intervals helps you navigate the fretboard with confidence, allowing you to explore different melodic possibilities.
- **Emotional Expression:** Each scale has a distinct emotional quality, and selecting the right scale can convey the desired mood in your improvisation. For instance, major scales often evoke happiness and brightness, while minor scales can express melancholy and introspection.
- **Technical Proficiency:** Practicing scales enhances your technical skills, such as finger dexterity, speed, and accuracy. These skills are essential for executing intricate passages and complex improvisational ideas.

Practical Techniques for Improvisation

1. Scale Familiarization

- **Practice Scales in Different Positions:** Practice playing scales in multiple positions on the fretboard. This will increase your familiarity with the neck and allow for greater flexibility in your improvisation.

- **Explore Scale Variations:** Experiment with different scales, such as major, minor, pentatonic, and modal scales. Each one offers unique sounds and possibilities for improvisation.

2. Connecting Scales with Chords

- **Chord Tone Targeting**: Focus on landing on chord tones during your improvisation. This creates a strong connection between your melodies and the chord progression, resulting in more coherent solos.

- **Arpeggios:** Incorporate arpeggios into your improvisation. Arpeggios highlight chord tones and provide a melodic path that complements the underlying harmony.

3. Composing Melodic Phrases

- **Motif Development:** Start with a simple melodic motif and develop it by altering its rhythm, dynamics, or phrasing. This creates variation and interest in your solos.

- **Call and Response**: Use the call-and-response technique to create a dialogue between different musical phrases. This adds depth and structure to your improvisation.

4. Experimenting with Rhythms

- **Syncopation and Polyrhythms:** Explore syncopated rhythms and polyrhythms to add complexity and excitement to your improvisation. These rhythmic variations can transform a simple scale into a captivating musical statement.

- **Dynamic Variation:** Employ dynamic changes within your solos to convey emotion and build tension or release. This keeps your audience engaged and adds expression to your playing.

By using scales as a foundation for improvisation, you'll unlock new dimensions of musical expression and creativity.

Lesson 27: Developing Melodic Phrases

Developing melodic phrases is a key aspect of crafting solos that captivate and engage listeners. While scales provide the foundation for your improvisation, the artistry lies in how you use these notes to create meaningful and expressive musical statements.

Melodic phrasing involves shaping a series of notes into coherent and expressive musical ideas. Much like a sentence in spoken language, a melodic phrase has a beginning, middle, and end.

It conveys emotion and intent. By focusing on phrasing, you can transform simple scale patterns into compelling musical narratives.

In this lesson, we will explore techniques for developing melodic phrases that will elevate your solos and help you communicate your musical ideas more effectively.

Such things as hammer-ons, pull-offs, bends, slides, vibrato, and guitar licks. All are used to develop melodic phrasing.

84

Hammer-on: Pick a note, and hammer-on to the next.

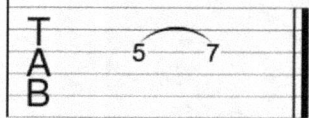

In this example, you pick the 5th fret on the 3rd string, and hammer-on to the 7th fret. A very common approach to playing the melody on the guitar.

Pull-off: Pick a note, and pull-off to the one behind it.

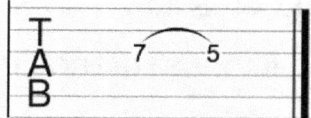

In this example, you do the opposite. You strike the note and pull-off to the one behind it. With this technique, you will need two fingers down on the same string. One to pick, and the other to pull-off to.

Slides: Pick a note, and slide to the next

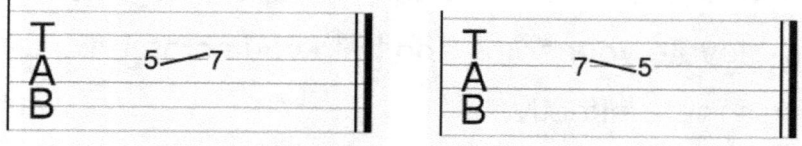

In these examples, you pick the note at the 5th fret, 3rd string, and slide up to the 7th fret, and then slide back down by doing the opposite.

String bend: You pick a note, and bend it to another note.

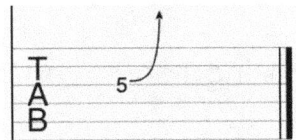

In this example, you pick the note on the 5th fret, 3rd string, and bend it to the next note.

Vibrato: Pick a note and slightly vibrate it up and down.

In this example, you pick the note at the 7th fret, 3rd string, and slightly vibrate it up and down.

Hammer-on, pull-off: Hammer-on and then pull-off.

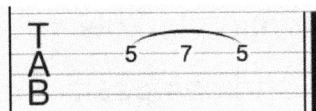

In this example, you pick the 5th fret, 3rd string, hammer-on to the 7th fret, and then pull back off to the 5th fret. All in one motion. Pick one note, but play three.

*These techniques, and more, will be the foundation of how you create melody with the scales and modes.

Lesson 28: Developing Your Own Style

Developing a personal style is a journey that distinguishes you as a guitarist. It's about integrating your influences, preferences, and creativity into a cohesive musical voice.

Scales and modes are fundamental in this process, serving as the building blocks that shape your sound.

This lesson will guide you in using scales to forge your unique style, drawing from your musical experiences and aspirations.

Integrating Scales into Your Style

1. Identify Your Influences

- **Analyze Your Favorites:** Listen to guitarists you admire and analyze their use of scales. Pay attention to how they incorporate scales into their solos, riffs, and compositions.
- **Draw Inspiration:** Identify elements from your favorite players that resonate with you. These could be specific scales, phrasing techniques, or tonal qualities.

2. Experiment with Scale Variations

- **Blend Different Scales:** Experiment by combining elements from various scales, such as mixing pentatonic with modal scales, to create hybrid sounds that reflect your musical tastes.

- **Alter Intervals:** Modify traditional scales by altering intervals to evoke different emotions or add a novel twist to your playing.

3. Develop Signature Motifs

- **Create Personal Licks:** Develop signature licks or motifs using your preferred scales. These can serve as recurring themes in your solos and compositions, adding a personal touch to your music.

- **Explore Rhythmic Variations:** Experiment with different rhythmic patterns to give your motifs a distinctive feel. Syncopation, odd time signatures, and dynamic phrasing can set your style apart.

This journey of self-discovery will not only enhance your guitar playing but also deepen your connection to music and your overall mastery of it.

Lesson 29: Improvisational Challenges

To develop your improvisational skills, it's essential to challenge yourself with exercises that push your boundaries, encourage new ideas, and allow you to think on your feet.

Here are improvisational challenges designed to enhance your ability to think on your feet and craft compelling solos.

1. Thematic Exploration

- **Pick a Theme:** Select a simple theme or motif to base your improvisation on. This could be a rhythmic pattern, a melodic fragment, or a specific emotion.
- **Develop Variations:** Improvise using the theme as a foundation. Create variations by altering rhythm, dynamics, and articulation, while maintaining the core idea.
- **Develop Variations:** Improvise using the theme as a foundation. Create variations by altering rhythm and dynamics, while maintaining the core idea.

2. Limitation Exercises

- **Note Limitation:** Restrict yourself to using only a few notes from a chosen scale. This encourages creativity within constraints and forces you to focus on phrasing and expression.

- **Rhythmic Limitation:** Limit your improvisation to using specific rhythmic patterns. Experiment with syncopation, rests, and polyrhythms to add complexity and interest.

3. Modal Exploration

- **Mode Switching:** Practice improvising by switching between different modes within the same key. This expands your harmonic vocabulary and introduces new tonal colors.

- **Contrast and Comparison:** Improvise using two contrasting modes, such as Ionian and Phrygian, to explore their distinct emotional qualities.

- **Modal Extensions:** Create phrasing that moves between multiple modes. This will enhance the overall tone and expression of the melody.

Tips for Embracing Improvisational Challenges

- **Stay Open to Mistakes:** Embrace mistakes as opportunities for growth and discovery. They often lead to unexpected and rewarding musical avenues.

- **Cultivate Curiosity:** Approach each improvisational challenge with curiosity and a willingness to experiment. This mindset encourages exploration and innovation.

- **Reflect on Progress:** Regularly assess your progress and set new challenges to continue expanding your improvisational skills.

- **Exchange Ideas:** Share improvisational ideas with fellow musicians and learn from their approaches. This exchange fosters support.

- **Practice Daily:** Only through daily practice will you be able to unlock the power of improvisation with scales and modes.

By embracing these improvisational challenges, you'll enhance your ability to craft spontaneous riffs, solos, and melody lines that will enrich your overall musical expression.

Lesson 30: Chapter 6 Quiz

These will reinforce your understanding of this chapter.

Q: How do scales serve as a foundation for improvisation?
A: _____

Q: What benefits do they provide when crafting guitar solos?
A: _____

Q: What are the key elements of melodic phrasing?
A: _____

Q: What steps can you take to develop a personal style?
A: _____

Q: How can you use scales to develop your unique sound?
A: _____

Q: List two improvisational challenges that can help you?
A: _____

Q: How do exercises encourage creativity in crafting solos?
A: _____

Remember, this is for your benefit, so have fun with it.

Chapter 6 Summary

In this chapter, we dive into the importance of improvisation and how you can use it as a foundation for creative expression. Remember, scales are the foundation of improvisation.

First, you learn how scales can provide the melodic and harmonic framework for crafting cohesive solos. To match the mood and context of your musical landscapes.

Second, you learned about melodic phrasing. Key elements such as hammer-ons, pull-offs, slides, etc, to shape your solos into meaningful musical statements.

Third, you learn about ways to use scales and improvising to develop your own sound.

Fourth, this chapter, and make sure you fully understand the concepts I have taught you in it. They will help you expand your knowledge of chords played further up the fretboard.

Lastly, you are presented with another learning assessment. This will help you retain the concepts within this lesson and help you gain confidence in these concepts.

Chapter 7 The Blues Scales

Lesson 31: The Major Blues Scale

The major blues scale is a versatile and expressive scale that fits seamlessly into the realms of rock and blues music. Known for its distinctive, moody sound.

It provides a unique blend of major and bluesy tones, making it an essential tool for guitarists looking to add flavor and character to their solos and compositions.

The major blues scale is an extension of the major pentatonic scale, incorporating an additional note known as the "blue" note. This note is the flattened 3rd, and adds a touch of tension and color, giving the scale its characteristic bluesy sound.

Since it is an extension of the major pentatonic scale, it will be easy to learn. Let's take a look.

C Major Pentatonic Scale: C D E G A = 1 2 3 5 6

C Major Blues Scale: C D Eb E G A = 1 2 b3 3 5 6

The Major Blues Scale

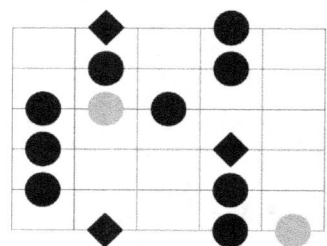

Since it is an extension of the major pentatonic scale, it is easy to learn since we already know most of it. We just need to add the flat 3rd note in the correct position.

Look closely and compare it to the major pentatonic scale. You will see that this note resides in two places. By adding this extra note, you create a different shade of color.

If the major pentatonic scale were the color royal blue, the major blues scale could be considered navy blue.

They are both the color blue, just different shades that bring about different emotions. The blues scale will always bring out a darker tone due to the added note.

Play this at the 8th fret and you have the C major blues scale. This concept can be done with all the pentatonic scale patterns.

Lesson 32: The Minor Blues Scale

The minor blues scale is a fundamental tool in the world of rock, blues, and jazz guitar playing. Known for its expressiveness and emotional depth, this scale is a staple for guitarists looking to add a soulful and gritty edge to their music.

Once again, just like the major blues scale, the minor blues scale is an extension of the minor pentatonic scale. Except in this scale, we add the flat 5th note.

It is this flat 5th note, the "blue" note as they call it, that gives the scale a darker, moodier tone quality. Perfect for blues, rock, and jazz.

What is great about these scales and the pentatonics is that they are simple to play and have a wide variety of uses across multiple genres of music. Making them exceptional tools to have in your lead guitar toolbox.

A Minor Pentatonic Scale: A C D E G = 1 b3 4 5 b7

A Minor Blues Scale: A C D Eb E G = 1 b3 4 b5 5 b7

*It's these flat notes that make it different than the major.

The Minor Blues Scale

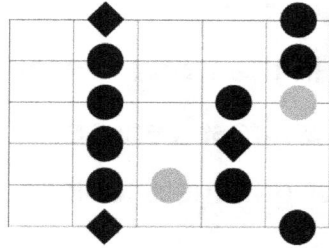

Since it is an extension of the minor pentatonic scale, it is easy to learn. All we need to do is add the flat 5th note in the correct position.

If you look closely and compare it to the minor pentatonic scale, you'll see that this note resides in two places, just like in the major blues scale. But in different locations.

Since this is so similar to the minor pentatonic scale, you could easily interchange the two. You can put the note in, or you can choose to leave it out, and since it is easy to play like the major, it has a very appealing nature.

The minor pentatonic, or the minor blues scale, is usually the first one guitarists learn when it comes to scales for playing guitar solos. Look to your favorite classic rock heroes; their solos are created with these scales.

Lesson 33: Blues Scale Patterns

As we've seen, the blues scales are an extension of the pentatonic scales. Both major and minor. This makes them extremely useful and easy to learn.

Since they are extensions of the pentatonics, they too have 5 scale patterns to choose from. Learning these will allow you to harness their full potential.

What's great is that even though you add a note, you don't need to add an extra pattern. You still work with just 5 of them for both the major and the minor.

C Major Blues Scale: C D Eb E G A

The flat 3rd note is simply added to the major pentatonic scale patterns to make the major blues scale.

A Minor Blues Scale: A C D Eb E G

With the minor blues scale, you add the flat 5th note to the scale patterns.

Remember, flat 3rd for the major, and flat 5th for the minor.

The 5 Major Blues Scale Patterns:

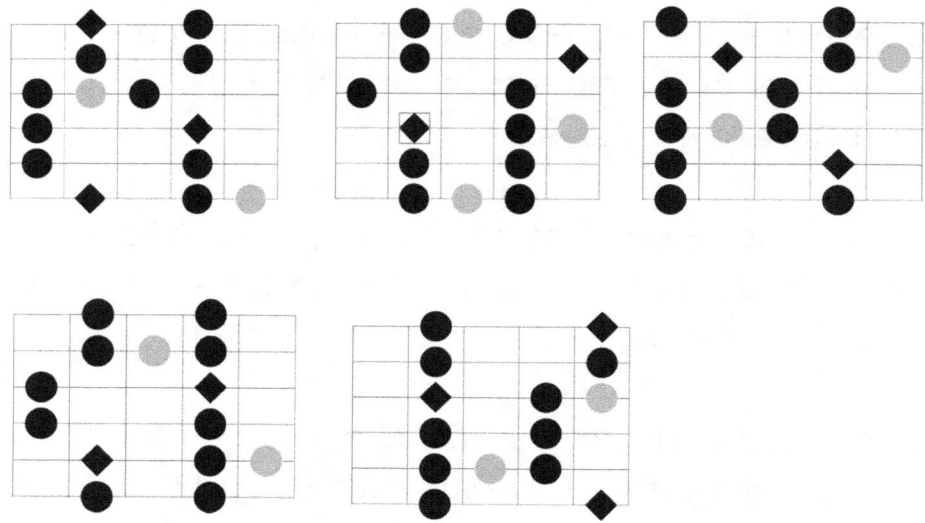

When looking at these scale patterns, you will notice, they are the same as the major pentatonic scale patterns, except for the "blue" note added. The flat 3rd.

This note can be added in 2 or more places in each scale pattern. This gives you more versatility to work with. Especially that by adding that note, you create a half step in certain areas of the scale.

It is these half steps, kind of like the modes, that give the scale patterns their unique tonal qualities. With each one sounding slightly different. Notice how the root note changes position in each one.

The 5 Minor Blues Scales

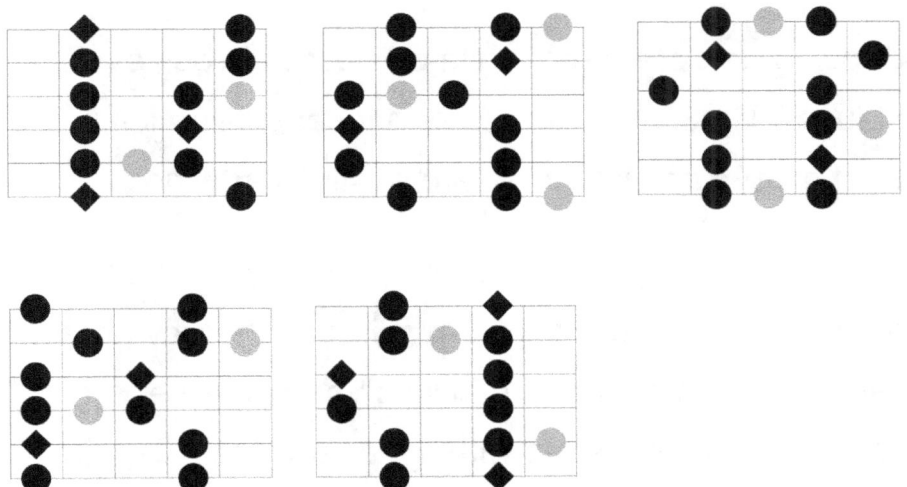

Like the major blues scale, the minor blues scale is an
extension of the minor pentatonic scale. With just one note
added. The flat 3rd. In the A minor blues scale, at the 5th fret,
this would be the E flat note.

As you can see from the diagram, this note in multiple places
expands the scale pattern. Allowing you to be more creative
with chromatic expressions in some scale patterns.

What is great about this scale pattern, along with the other
ones, is that even though the pattern changes location along
the fretboard (3rd fret, 5th fret, etc), the pattern stays the same.
Get these down in A minor, then practice them in other keys.

Lesson 34: Blues and Rock Applications

Blues and rock music are deeply related because rock evolved out of the blues. That is why there are a lot of similarities in both styles of music, and why they are easily intertwined.

When it comes to playing riffs, solos, and melody lines, scales play a pivotal role in both genres. Providing the framework that defines their distinctive sounds. Allowing you to create compelling, creative landscapes within these styles.

Blues Music

Blues music is created by its emotional phrasing, call-and-response patterns, and use of the "blue" notes, which add a certain tension and emotion to the music.

Thus making the major and minor blues scales fundamental to expressing creativity in this musical genre.

- **Major Blues Scale:** Has a nice uplifting tonal quality
- **Minor Blues Scale:** Has a dark, moody tonal quality

Both of these scales allow you to create emotional melody lines that easily cater to this style of music.

Rock Music

Rock music is slightly different, but not much. It is known for its energetic and powerful sound. Often featuring driving rhythms, catchy riffs, and dynamic solos and melody lines.

Since this is the case, the major and minor pentatonic scales are a staple widely used in this style of music, with the major having a bright tone and the minor having a somber tone.

As you can see from previous studies of these scale patterns, they can easily interchange with each other, but can also be played separately. This gives you a wide variety of options to choose from.

- **Major Pentatonic scale:** Bright uplifting tonal quality
- **Minor pentatonic Scale:** Sad, somber tonal quality

Both cater to elements used in rock music and can be chosen for creating these types of emotions in your music.

Both the pentatonic and blues scales are used for a variety of applications in both blues and rock music, you expand your abilities to create moving, emotional compositions.

102

Blues Applications

Create a simple blues lick using the minor blues scale. Focus on incorporating the blue note to enhance expression.

Play the lick over a 12-bar blues progression, experimenting with different rhythms and phrasing.

Develop a call-and-response pattern using the major or minor blues scale.

Integrate this pattern into your improvisation over a blues backing track, emphasizing dynamic contrasts.

Rock Applications

Use the minor pentatonic scale to create a driving rock riff. Focus on rhythm and repetition to build intensity.

Play the riff with a metronome, gradually increasing the tempo to enhance precision and speed.

Improvise a solo using the Mixolydian mode. Incorporate techniques like bends, slides, and vibrato for added expression.

These exercises, and more like them, will allow you to develop a full understanding and the use of these scales in both blues and rock music.

Lesson 35: Chapter 7 Quiz

Chapter 7 deals with scales that are very popular in many songs. The blues scales. Make sure to study and put into practice these lessons. You will not regret it.

Q: What is the "blue" note in the C major blues scale?
A: _____

Q: What type of emotion does the major blues scale convey?
A: _____

Q: What notes make up the C major blues scale?
A: _____

Q: What notes make up the A minor blues scale?
A: _____

Q: Why are the blues scales different from the pentatonics?
A: _____

Q: What scales are best used for blues music?
A: _____

Q: What scales are best used for rock music?
A: _____

Chapter 7 Summary

In this chapter, you have learned about the blues scales. These are very similar to the pentatonic scales and can be easily combined for a wider variety of creative possibilities.

<u>First</u>, you start with the major blues scale. To create this scale, you just add the flat 3rd note to the major pentatonic scale. In the C major blues scale, this would be E flat.

<u>Second</u>, you learned about the minor blues scale, and to create this, you add the flat 5th note to the minor pentatonic scale. In A minor, this would be the E flat note as well.

<u>Third</u>, you learned about the blues scale patterns. Since they are so closely related to the pentatonics, you just add the notes mentioned above to those five patterns.

<u>Fourth</u>, you learned about applications that these scales can be used for in both blues and rock music. With exercise ideas for enhancing your use of them.

<u>Lastly</u>, you are presented with a brief quiz to make sure you fully understand the chapter. I recommend you do not skip these, as they are for your benefit.

Chapter 8: Effective Scale Practice

Lesson 36: Effective Practice Methods

Mastering guitar scales is a journey that demands dedication and strategic practice. Efficient practice methods can enhance your technical skills and deepen your understanding.

Establish a Practice Routine

- **Set clear goals**: Begin each session with a specific goal in mind. Like improving speed and accuracy.
- **Time management:** Allocate dedicated time to scale practice within your routine.
- **Warm-up Exercises**: These prepare your fingers, wrists, and hands for the upcoming activity.

Focused Scale Practice

- **Scale Isolation:** Work on one individual scale at a time. This will help you to fully master it.
- **Tempo Variation:** Use a metronome and practice scales at different tempos.
- **Position shifts:** Practice scales in various positions across the fretboard.

Maintain Motivation and Enjoyment

Maintaining motivation and enjoyment in learning the guitar is crucial. Here are some pointers that can help.

- **Set Milestones:** Celebrate achievements along the way. Even small ones will keep you motivated and having fun.
- **Explore Variety:** Explore different styles and techniques to keep learning fresh and interesting.
- **Track Your Progress:** This will let you know what you have accomplished and what you still need to work on.
- **Record and Review:** This technique allows you to visualize your progress from an outside point of view.
- **Have fun:** Make sure to have fun. Don't allow stress to creep in. Enjoy the journey and celebrate your progress.

By implementing these effective practice methods, you'll make the most of your practice sessions. In doing so, you'll enhance your proficiency.

Remember, the key to progress is consistent, focused practice combined with a passion for learning and discovery. Embrace these strategies through daily study and practice, and your guitar skills will reach a new level.

Lesson 37: Speed and Accuracy Drills

Mastering speed and accuracy on the guitar is a common goal for many players, as it enhances both technical proficiency and expressive potential.

This lesson focuses on targeted exercise ideas designed to help you increase your playing speed while maintaining precision.

By incorporating these drills into your practice routine, you'll develop the skills needed to tackle complex pieces and execute intricate solos with confidence.

Chromatic Exercises

The purpose of chromatic exercises is to develop finger independence while increasing speed across the fretboard.

Scale Runs

The purpose of scale runs is to familiarize yourself with the note intervals of the scales and improve fluidity across the fretboard.

108

String Skipping

The purpose of string skipping is to develop precision and control when moving across multiple strings.

Alternate picking

The purpose of alternate picking is to increase speed and accuracy. Best done with a metronome.

Lagato Techniques

The purpose of legato techniques is to improve smoothness and fluidity across the fretboard with repeated hammer-ons.

Tremolo Picking

The purpose of tremolo picking is to double-time your alternate picking. Once you get alternate down, work on tremolo picking.

By incorporating these speed and accuracy drills into your practice routine, you'll enhance your technical proficiency and unlock endless possibilities in your guitar playing.

Embrace the challenge, stay patient, and enjoy the journey of becoming a more skilled and versatile guitarist. When it's all said and done, you'll be glad you did.

Lesson 38: Ear Training with Scales

Ear training is an essential component of musicianship, enhancing your ability to recognize pitches, intervals, and harmonies.

By incorporating ear training exercises into your scale practice, you can develop a more intuitive understanding of music, helping you play confidently and creatively.

Importance of Ear Training

- **Improved Pitch Recognition**: Accurately identify pitches of notes within scales and chords.
- **Memory Retention:** Allows you to remember harmonies and melodies more effectively.
- **Enhanced Communication:** Allows you to communicate more effectively with other musicians.
- **Transcribe Melodies:** This allows you to listen to melodies and reproduce them by ear.

By training your ear, you'll be able to develop a more intuitive and confident approach to music without needing sheet music.

Techniques for Ear Training with Scales

Singing Scales

- **Vocal Practice**: Sing the notes of a scale while playing them on your guitar. Focus on matching pitch accurately and maintaining a steady rhythm.
- **Interval Recognition**: Sing intervals within the scale, such as thirds, fourths, and fifths. This helps you internalize the sound of different intervals and their relationships.

Interval Training

- **Interval Identification**: Practice identifying intervals within a scale by ear. Start with simple intervals and gradually progress to more complex ones.
- **Interval Singing**: Sing different intervals and play them on your guitar to reinforce your understanding of their sound and structure.

These exercises will enhance your ability to recognize and respond to musical elements, enriching your overall musicianship and creative expression.

Lesson 39: Integrating Scales with Chords

This lesson focuses on techniques for harmonizing scales within chords, providing a deeper understanding of their relationship and practical applications.

The ability to seamlessly integrate scales with chords is a vital skill for any guitarist, enhancing both compositional and improvisational capabilities.

Understanding how scales and chords interact allows you to create more cohesive and expressive music.

Relationship Between Chords & Scales

Chords are built from the notes of a scale, sharing common tones. By identifying these, you can choose scales that complement the harmony of a progression.

Highlighting chords (the root, third, fifth, and sometimes the seventh) within a scale ensures your melodies align properly.

This allows you to create solos with confidence, knowing that they align harmoniously with the chords underneath them.

Harmonizing Scales and Chords

Match each chord in a progression with a corresponding scale. For example, use the C major scale over a C major chord and the A minor scale over an A minor chord.

Practice improvising by switching scales as the chords change. Focus on making smooth transitions between scales to maintain melodic continuity.

Pay attention to how scales and chords interact in your favorite songs. To how notes of scales are used to enhance chords and progressions.

When you create chords and chord progressions from the key of C major, you can see that a solo in C major pentatonic will fit nicely with it. Remember, this works with minor keys as well.

Key of C Major: C D E F G A B: For playing harmony

C Major Pentatonic: C D E G A: For playing melody

By mastering the integration of scales and chords, you'll gain the ability to craft music that is both creative and engaging. This knowledge will empower you to add depth and expression to your guitar playing.

Lesson 40: Chapter 8 Quiz

Once again, we have a simple assessment exercise (or quiz) to make sure you know the material in this chapter.

Q: What are some key strategies for effective scale practice?
A: _____

Q: What two exercises can improve your speed and accuracy?
A: _____

Q: How can scales be used to develop your ear training?
A: _____

Q: What is the relationship between scales and chords?
A: _____

Q: Why is it important to have a practice routine?
A: _____

By answering these questions, you'll reinforce your understanding of these concepts. Put them into practice daily, and your guitar playing will reach new heights.

114

Chapter 8 Summary

In this final chapter, you have learned about effective scale practice. Concepts and techniques that can deepen your understanding of guitar scales.

If applied daily with dedication and persistence, your musicianship will grow, along with your mastery over the fretboard.

<u>First</u>, you learn to establish a practice routine and learn ways to stay motivated and continue to make the journey enjoyable. Without this, you won't stick with it.

<u>Second</u>, you learn concepts for increasing speed and accuracy to enhance your technical proficiency and unlock unlimited possibilities in your guitar playing.

<u>Third</u>, you learned about how scales can improve your ear training. Concepts and techniques that will allow you to replicate notes without the need for sheet music.

<u>Fourth</u>, you learned about integrating scales with chords. This knowledge will allow you to create solos that fit harmoniously with the chords and their progressions.

Learn Guitar Scale Theory Conclusion

Congratulations on completing your journey through guitar scale theory! With the knowledge and skills gained from this book, you're now prepared to explore new musical horizons and deepen your connection to the guitar.

Remember, the key to mastery is practice, patience, and a passion for continuous learning. Keep playing, keep experimenting, and most importantly, enjoy the music you create.

As you continue to develop as a guitarist, remember that the scales and theories you've learned are just the beginning. They are tools that will help you express your creativity and explore the vast landscape of musical possibilities.

Whether you're composing, improvising, or simply enjoying the act of playing, these scales will serve as a foundation for your musical journey. Use them to craft your own voice, and don't hesitate to push the boundaries of what you know.

Music is a universal language, and your guitar is a powerful means of communication. Embrace the diversity of sounds and styles available to you, and always remain open to new influences and ideas.

As you grow as a musician, you will inevitably encounter challenges, but each challenge is an opportunity for growth. Keep pushing your limits, and let your passion for music guide you through each new phase of your artistic evolution.

If you find value in this book, please do let me know by leaving a review. Or, if you have any questions about any lessons, be sure to let me know, and I will be happy to assist you.

Be sure to follow me on Instagram, Facebook, etc, and visit my website for more information on my lessons.

DwaynesGuitarLessons.com

Best of luck and have fun.

Sincerely, Dwayne Jenkins
Tritone Publishing. Copyright © 2025

Other Books By Dwayne's Guitar Lessons

Lead Guitar Shredder

A beginner's guide to playing shred guitar.   A perfect compliment to guitar scale theory. Teaching you advanced techniques and concepts utilizing scales.

A comprehensive method book on the art of shred guitar. You'll learn to read notation, increasing your speed and accuracy, sweep pick, finger tapping, legato, and much, much more.

Learn Guitar Chord Theory

A comprehensive method book on creating guitar chords. For students with no previous musical background. With lesson examples presented in today's most popular step-by-step format.

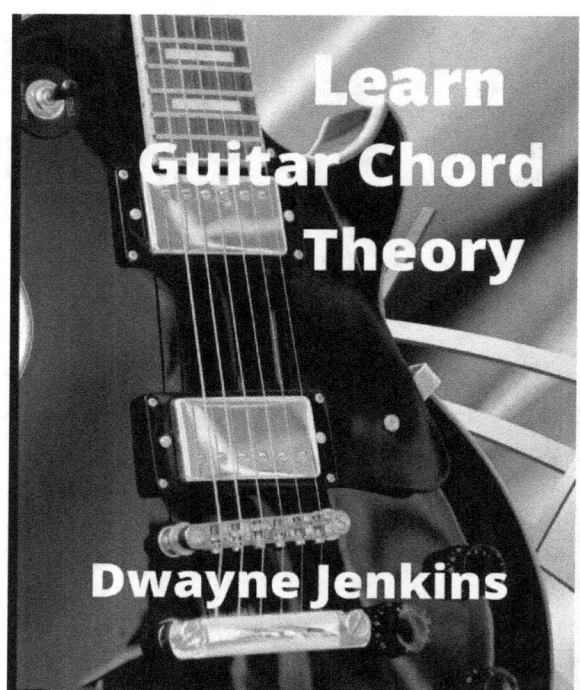

A perfect complementary book to Learn Guitar Scale Theory. Showing you all about how guitar chords are created, and how to use them to enhance your musicianship.

Electric Guitar 101

If you are just getting started on the electric guitar, this book will provide you with everything you need to build a solid foundation.

Packed with photos, diagrams, easy-to-read and understand notation, step-by-step lessons, learning assessments, and much, much more. You'll be playing guitar in no time.

All books by Dwayne Jenkins can be found in print and digital formats for your convenience. Available worldwide, where all books are sold.

These can also be found on Dwayne's website in digital format for quicker learning. Just download it onto your computer and start learning right away.

Online courses are also available with video instruction, assignments, and assessments to make sure you fully understand the material.

Self-study is a great way to learn, as it allows you to not only go at your own pace but also develop the skills of discipline and time management. These things can benefit you in other areas of your life as well.

If more help is needed, Dwayne also offers one-on-one private coaching. Which can also be found on his website.

www.dwaynesguitarlessons.com.

Also, be sure to check out Dwayne's video lessons on YouTube. These are free and available 24 hours a day, 7 days a week, 365 days a year. They cover a wide range of topics to help you excel in your learning.

About the Author

Dwayne Jenkins is a professional guitar teacher, an accomplished musician, and an entrepreneur. He has been learning, playing, and teaching guitar lessons throughout Denver, CO, for over two decades.

He is now bringing his special training skills and methodology that have been honed and hand-crafted throughout the years on how to play to students around the world.

Dwayne has a unique, exciting approach that gets students of all ages and skill levels enjoying the fun of playing guitar and ukulele. His enthusiasm and love for teaching shine through with every lesson that he creates.

His lessons are designed to enhance your ability to progress. No matter your reason for learning, there will always be something in Dwayne's books and products to help you achieve your dreams.

So if you're a student looking to start, or a student looking to further your education, be sure to get involved with Dwayne's guitar lessons and discover why learning to play the guitar is one of the greatest things you can do for yourself.

Guitar Scale Guide

The 3 Minor Scales: Natural, Harmonic & Melodic

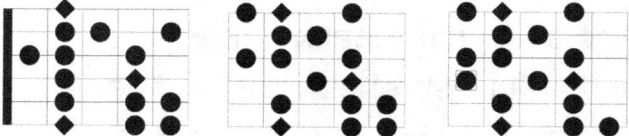

The 5 Major Pentatonic Scale Patterns

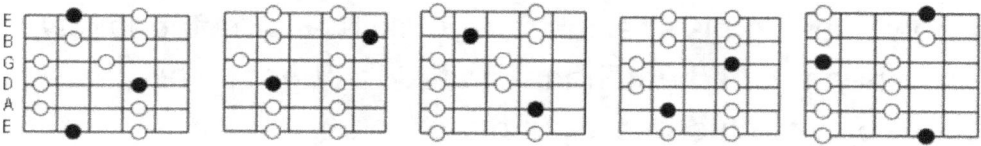

The 5 Minor Pentatonic Scale Patterns

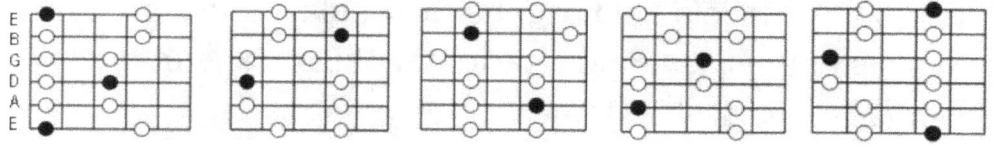

The 7 Modes of the Major Scale

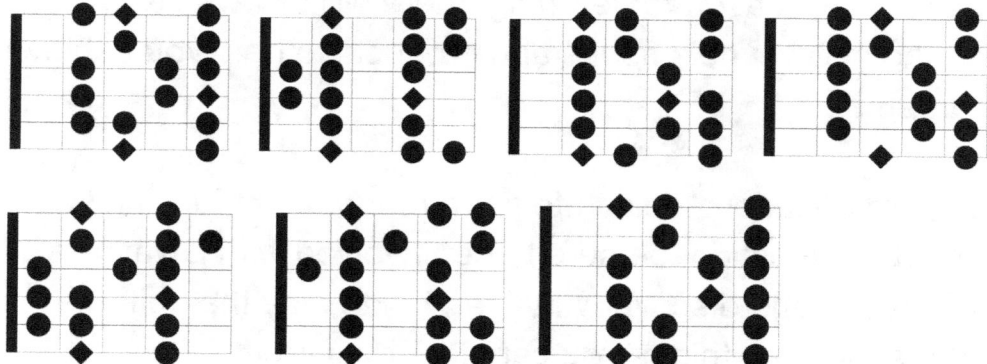

Guitar Scale Guide Continued

The 5 Major Blues Scales

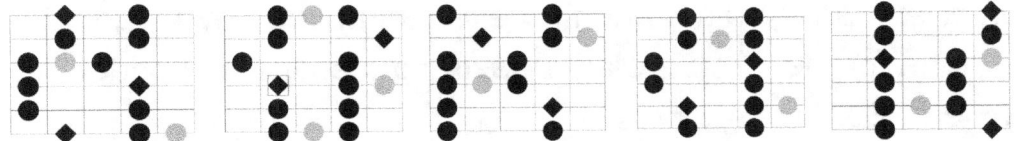

The 5 Minor Blues Scales

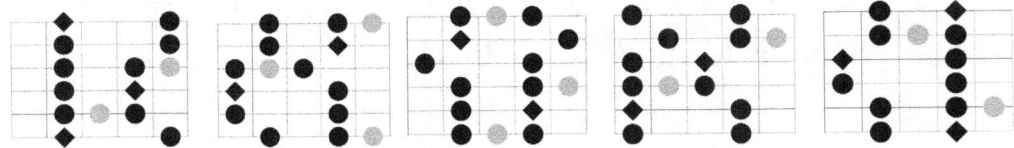

Natural Minor = 1 2 b3 4 5 b6 b7
Harmonic Minor = 1 2 b3 4 5 b6 7
Melodic Minor = 1 2 b3 4 5 6 7

Major Pentatonic = 1 2 3 5 6
Minor Pentatonic = 1 2 b3 4 5 b7

Ionian = 1 2 3 4 5 6 7   **Dorian** = 1 2 b3 4 5 6 b7
Phrygian = 1 b2 b3 4 5 b6 b7   **Lydian** = 1 2 3 #4 5 6 7
Mixolydian = 1 2 3 4 5 6 b7   **Aeolian** = 1 2 b3 4 5 b6 b7
Locrian = 1 b2 b3 4 b5 b6 b7

Major Blues Scale = 1 2 b3 3 5 6
Minor Blues Scale = 1 b3 4 b5 5 b7

What Students Are Saying About Dwayne's Guitar Lessons

"Dwayne, thank you so much for everything you have taught me and done for me. You are an amazing guitarist and wonderful teacher," BJ.

"Dwayne, it has been a true pleasure to have you at our house each week! Ken & Trevor have learned so much through you and your teachings. Thank you!" Lisa

"Dwayne, thank you for being a great teacher and teaching me many great songs. This is a skill that will last me a lifetime." Danielle

"Dwayne, we want you to know we are honored to have you at the studio. We appreciate all that you do and are grateful that we can leave you in charge." Angie & Wilson M.E.C.

"Dwayne, we are so glad you are our Teacher. It's been three years already, can you believe it? Thank you again. You're the best!" Chelsey & Lucas.

"Dwayne, we are so glad that you are in our lives. Chelsey & Lucas enjoy their time with you and look up to you. Looking forward to another great year!" Love and best wishes, Ken & Sue.

"Dwayne, thank you so much for being not only an awesome guitar teacher, but an awesome friend as well," Kayla.

"Dwayne, thank you so much for all the years of doing lessons. You have been very patient with my progress, helped me to build confidence in myself, and inspired me to follow my dreams. And in doing so, you have become a great friend," Jake.

"Dwayne, thank you so much for teaching me every Saturday and not only teaching me guitar but also about life, and helping me with setting my goals. You are a great teacher, mentor, and the best friend ever," Carson.

"There is no other person I would want to be teaching me a guitar! His 1-on-1 teaching makes learning guitar very personal & exhilarating. He teaches at your pace and takes pride in what YOU want to learn. The best part...if Dwayne doesn't know a song a student wants to play, he takes time out of the week to learn it. His teaching comes to life in my performance and has progressed over the last 8 years. Words cannot describe how amazing a teacher, rockstar, and true friend Dwayne has become to me," Dominic.

Thanks again for your time.

Blank Diagrams For Writing Out Guitar Scales

*Writing them out helps to imprint them on your brain.